Intermediate

Complete Communication

James Bury **Anthony Sellick** **Kaori Horiuchi**

BOOK

2

SEIBIDO

音声ファイルのダウンロード／ストリーミング

CD マーク表示がある箇所は、音声を弊社 HP より無料でダウンロード／ストリーミングすることができます。下記 URL の書籍詳細ページに音声ダウンロードアイコンがございますのでそちらから自習用音声としてご活用ください。

http://seibido.co.jp/ad635

PREFACE

In today's global society it is becoming increasingly important to be able to communicate in a wide range of contexts. This includes talking and writing about different topics, interacting with different people, and building knowledge of vocabulary in order to express opinions and justify them.

Complete Communication is a new series of textbooks that aims to develop students' overall communication skills, incorporating both receptive and productive activities. *Complete Communication Book 2 – Intermediate –* is the second book in the series.

Each of the fifteen units in the *Complete Communication Book 2 – Intermediate –* student book looks at a specific topic that people will encounter regularly, whether in everyday conversations or in more formal situations, such as examinations. The topics range from music and health to culture and future plans.

Each unit follows a set plan and incorporates easy to follow activities. There are opportunities to learn and practice vocabulary in each unit as well as activities that focus on the gist and the details of listening texts. Each unit also incorporates three speaking activities that can be used in a controlled manner and sections which help with pronunciation and grammar. Each unit is also accompanied by two activities in the appendix that encourage further extended speaking and writing.

In addition to helping build students' knowledge of communicative English by providing practice for the core language needed to interact effectively in pair conversations and small group discussions, this series has been developed to enhance students' self-perceptions of ability and levels of confidence when using English. By doing this, it is hoped that students will come to see learning English as fulfilling, engaging, and fun, and that English is a language of communication and interaction in real-world situations, not just a language to be studied for tests.

We hope that you will find the topics and activities interesting and thought-provoking, and that they encourage you to learn more about successful communication strategies and techniques. We sincerely hope you enjoy studying and working through *Complete Communication*.

James Bury, Anthony Sellick, and Kaori Horiuchi

CONTENTS

CONTENT CHART

Focus on Function	Communication Outcomes
Using *shall we* and *let's* to make and respond to suggestions	Be able to ask for and provide personal information
Using *that sounds* to react and give opinions	Be able to ask for and provide information about hobbies and pastimes
Confirmation of understanding	Be able to ask for and provide information about friends and family
Using *I don't mind* to express preference and willingness	Be able to ask for and provide information and opinions about movies and TV shows
Using *when* and *since*	Be able to ask for and provide information and opinions about playing and enjoying music
Using *I wish I could* to express desire	Be able to ask for and provide information and opinions about reading
Using *could you* to make requests	Be able to ask for and provide information and opinions about food and drink
Using *once* as a time marker	Be able to ask for and provide information and opinions about sports, exercise, and health
Using *not sure* to express doubt and uncertainty	Be able to ask for and provide information and opinions about health and illness
Using *be supposed to*	Be able to ask for and provide information and opinions about culture and customs
Prepositions of time	Be able to ask for and provide information and opinions about holidays and festivals
Using *must*	Be able to ask for and provide information and opinions about travel and vacations
Using *I'd rather* to express preference	Be able to ask for and provide information and opinions about past experiences
Using *that's why*	Be able to ask for and provide information and opinions about work and jobs
Using *feel like*	Be able to ask for and provide information and opinions about future plans

EnglishCentralのご案内

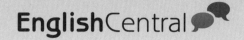

本テキスト各ユニットの「III. Conversation : Part 2」と「IV. Pronunciation Check : Exercises」で学習する音声は、オンライン学習システム「EnglishCentral」で学習することができます。

EnglishCentralでは動画の視聴や単語のディクテーションのほか、動画のセリフを音読し録音すると、コンピュータが発音を判定します。PCのwebだけでなく、スマートフォン、タブレットではアプリでも学習できます。リスニング、スピーキング、語彙力向上のため、ぜひ活用してください。

EnglishCentralの利用にはアカウントとアクセスコードの登録が必要です。登録方法については下記ページにアクセスしてください。

（画像はすべてサンプルで、実際の教材とは異なります）

https://www.seibido.co.jp/englishcentral/pdf/ectextregister.pdf

見る

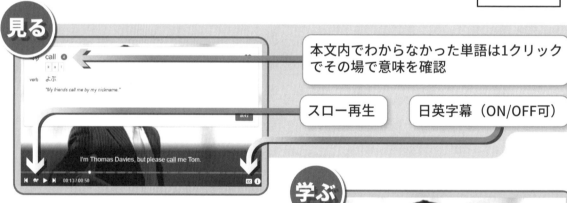

本文内でわからなかった単語は1クリックでその場で意味を確認

スロー再生

日英字幕（ON/OFF可）

学ぶ

音声を聴いて空欄の単語をタイピング。ゲーム感覚で楽しく単語を覚える

話す

動画のセリフを音読し録音、コンピュータが発音を判定。

日本人向けに専門開発された音声認識によってスピーキング力を％で判定

ネイティブと自分が録音した発音を聞き比べ練習に生かすことができます

苦手な発音記号を的確に判断し、単語を緑、黄、赤の3色で表示

UNIT 1

It's good to meet you.
– Introducing Yourself

I | Vocabulary

Part 1: Match the words and phrases (a~j) with their meanings (1~10).

a. describe	b. hometown	c. prefecture	d. grow up	e. country
f. personality	g. rural	h. urban	i. freshman	j. sophomore

1. _____ the place you come from
2. _____ characteristics
3. _____ a student in the first year of college or university
4. _____ a student in the second year of college or university
5. _____ to mature, to become an adult
6. _____ a state, a nation
7. _____ built-up area, like a city or town
8. _____ not built-up area, like the countryside
9. _____ to explain, give details about
10. _____ an area within a country

Part 2: Complete the dialogs with words and phrases from Part 1.

1. **A:** Where are you from?
   B: My _____ is Kobe. It's a great city.
2. **A:** Which _____ are you from?
   B: I'm from Nepal. It's between China and India.
3. **A:** How would you _____ yourself?
   B: That's difficult! People say I have a relaxed personality.
4. **A:** Have you always lived in a city like Tokyo?
   B: No, I used to live in a(n) _____ area in Gifu.
5. **A:** Are you a new student at this university?
   B: Yes, I'm a(n) _____. Today's my first day.

2, 3

Listening Practice: Listen to two people making short introductions. Write the speakers' names and check (✔) the correct boxes.

1. Name: _____

	Yes	No
is Japanese	☐	☐
lives in a city	☐	☐
is a freshman	☐	☐
is shy	☐	☐

2. Name: _____

	Yes	No
is Japanese	☐	☐
lives in a city	☐	☐
is a freshman	☐	☐
is shy	☐	☐

Speaking Practice: What do you ask about when you first meet someone? Check the boxes below and talk to your partner about what they ask about.

	Yes	Sometimes	No	Reason
family	☐	☐	☐	_____
hometown	☐	☐	☐	_____
hobbies/pastimes	☐	☐	☐	_____
favorite food	☐	☐	☐	_____
favorite music	☐	☐	☐	_____

Useful Language

Questions
- Where do/did you live?
- What's your favorite . . . ?
- How would you describe yourself?

Answers
- I live in . . . / I used to live in . . .
- I like . . . / My favorite . . . is . . .
- I'm . . . / I have a(n) . . . personality.

Details
- Characteristics: pleasant / sociable / honest / active / considerate / sympathetic
- Areas: region / prefecture / country / rural / urban

Notes
I'm shy. / I'm a shy person.
人の性格を説明するとき、"I'm . . . / He is . . ." に形容詞を続けて表現する以外に、"I'm an idealist." のように be 動詞＋名詞の形で表現することもできます。"I'm a shy person." や "I have a passive personality." などの言い方も覚えておきましょう。

III ‖Conversation

 4

■ **Part 1:** Listen to the conversation and choose the most appropriate answer (a~d) for each question.

▌*Get the gist*

1. Who are Thomas and Reina most likely?

   a. Old school friends   **b.** Co-workers

   c. New classmates   **d.** Teacher and student

2. What is probably true about Thomas and Reina?

   a. They are freshman students.   **b.** They are sophomore students.

   c. They are university teachers.   **d.** They are visitors at the university.

▌*Get the details*

1. What course is Reina studying?

   a. International Communication   **b.** Business Management

   c. International Management   **d.** English Interaction

2. Why was Reina surprised?

   a. Because Thomas asked about Building B.

   b. Because Thomas is a new student.

   c. Because she studies the same course as Thomas.

   d. Because she is in the same first class as Thomas.

3. Who has studied with Mrs. Kanda before?

   a. Reina   **b.** One of Reina's friends

   c. Thomas   **d.** One of Thomas' friends

4. What does Thomas ask Reina to do?

   a. Be in his class   **b.** Study with him

   c. Tell him about Mrs. Kanda **d.** Go to their class together

Part 2: Listen to the conversation again and write the missing words or phrases in the spaces.

Thomas: Excuse me. Do you know where Building B is? It's my first day here and I'm

(1) _____ _____ _____ where to go.

Reina: Yes. This is Building B. It's my first day, too. There's a lot of information to

(2) _____, isn't there?

Thomas: Yes! (3) _____ _____ _____, my name's Thomas.

Reina: Hi, Thomas. I'm Reina. Nice to meet you. Which course are you

(4) _____?

Thomas: Nice to meet you, too. I'm on the International Communication course. My first

class is English Interaction. I'm quite nervous. (5) _____

_____ _____?

Reina: I'm studying the Business Management course, but my first class is English

Interaction as well. Who's your teacher?

Thomas: Hang on, let me quickly check . . . . Her name is Mrs. Kanda.

Reina: Oh, wow! She's my teacher! It sounds like we'll be in the same class! I heard

from my friend who studied with her last year that she's a great teacher. I think

we've been really lucky.

Thomas: That's good to (6) _____. I'm a little less nervous now. So, our class starts

soon. Shall we go there together?

Reina: Yes, let's do that. We can get to know each other a (7) _____ on the way.

Speaking Practice: Practice the conversation with your partner.

IV Pronunciation Check

強弱に注意しよう！

英語をネイティブスピーカーのように発音するには、強弱をつけてテンポよく話すことが大切です。大事な内容は強く、それ以外は弱く発音してみましょう。強弱のリズムに慣れることで、リスニング力も高まります。

基本的に、名詞、be 動詞以外の動詞、形容詞、副詞などを強く発音します。

例）My first class is English Interaction. 下線部の語が強く発音されています。

Exercises

 5

◢ Listen to the recording and underline the stressed words in the sentences below. Then, practice saying the sentences, paying attention to stress.

1. She is good at playing the piano.

2. I unexpectedly met Joe on the way to school.

3. Making a schedule is important to achieve your goals.

V Focus on Function

Shall we . . . ? / Let's . . . 「〜しましょう」

相手を何かに誘うときは、"Shall we . . . ?" や "Let's . . ." に動詞の原形を繋げて使います。助動詞の shall にはいくつかの意味がありますが、日常会話では "Shall we . . . ?" で勧誘を示す言い方が多く使われます。Let's は Let us が縮約されたもので、一緒に何かをすることを提案・勧誘する表現です。どちらの表現も賛成する場合は、"Yes, let's." や "Sure."、断る場合は、"No, let's not." や "Sorry, I can't." と答えましょう。

Exercises

◢ Complete the sentences below using *shall we* and *let's*.

1. 来週の土曜日に海へ行きませんか？
   _____ _____ _____ to the beach _____ Saturday ?

2. 一緒にテニスサークルに入ろうよ。
   _____ _____ a tennis club _____ .

3. あと 5 分で会議が始まります。そろそろ行きましょうか。
   The _____ starts in five minutes. _____ _____ get going?

VI ‖ Find out

📖 In the conversation on p.4, Thomas and Reina asked some questions to get to know each other. Think about some questions you can ask your classmates to get to know them and write them below. Then, write your answers to the questions. Finally, ask a partner the questions and find out about them.

Q1: (Where / from) _____ ?	
You: _____	Your partner: _____
Q2: (Where / grow up) _____ ?	
You: _____	Your partner: _____
Q3: (How many / people / family) _____ ?	
You: _____	Your partner: _____
Q4: (What / course / studying) _____ ?	
You: _____	Your partner: _____
Q5: (What / your favorite) _____ ?	
You: _____	Your partner: _____
Q6: Your question: _____ ?	
You: _____	Your partner: _____

Useful Language

Noun phrases: history / economics / political science / liberal arts / nursing / architecture / freshman / sophomore

Verb phrases: I'm studying . . . / I'm taking a/an . . . class. / I'm taking Prof. X's class. / I'm majoring in . . .

《何を勉強しているか話してみよう》

自己紹介のとき、自分が何を勉強しているか、専門分野やコースについて話してみましょう。「〜を勉強しています」という表現でも良いですし、受けている授業について話してみても良いでしょう。「授業を受ける」は take を使って表します。「専攻する」という意味の major を使うときは、"major in . . ." のように in の後ろに専攻分野を続けます。

例）I'm majoring in physics.（私は物理学を専攻しています）

UNIT 2

What are you into?
– Talking about Hobbies and Interests

I Vocabulary

Part 1: Match the words (a~j) with their meanings (1~10).

a. prefer	b. fan	c. interest	d. join	e. member
f. terrible	g. rarely	h. activity	i. never	j. occasionally

1. _____ not at any time
2. _____ a person or a part of a group or an organization
3. _____ to like (someone or something) better than someone or something else
4. _____ sometimes but not often
5. _____ something that is done as work or for a particular purpose
6. _____ hardly ever, almost never
7. _____ a person who really likes someone or something (like a celebrity, team, or group)
8. _____ a hobby or pastime that you enjoy learning about or doing
9. _____ very bad
10. _____ to become part of a group or organization

Part 2: Complete the dialogs with words from Part 1.

1. **A:** Is watching TV a hobby?
   B: No, it's a pastime. Hobbies and pastimes are both kinds of free time _____, but a hobby needs more effort. You're in the Baseball Club, so that's your hobby.
2. **A:** Can I help you?
   B: Yes, please. I'd like to _____ the Brass Band Club.
3. **A:** You look really tired. Are you okay?
   B: I had a(n) _____ weekend. All I did was study for today's test.
4. **A:** Can I take a photo with you, please? I'm a big _____ of your music.
   B: Sure, no problem. Smile!
5. **A:** Were you in any clubs when you were a high school student?
   B: Yes, I was. I was a(n) _____ of the English Club in junior high school, and the Debating Society in senior high school. What about you?

II ‖Warm-up for Listening & Speaking

 6, 7

■ **Listening Practice:** Listen to two people talking about things they like to do. Write the speakers' free time activities and check (✔) the correct boxes.

1. Free time activity: _____

	Yes	No
started six years ago	☐	✔
is in a club	☐	☐
is difficult	☐	☐
was a winner	☐	☐

2. Free time activity: _____

	Yes	No
started six years ago	☐	☐
is in a club	☐	☐
is difficult	☐	☐
was a winner	☐	☐

■ **Speaking Practice:** What kind of free time activities are important to you? Check the boxes below and talk to your partner about their free time activities.

	Very important	Quite important	Not important	Reason
internet surfing	☐	☐	☐	_____
listening to music	☐	☐	☐	_____
playing sports	☐	☐	☐	_____
playing games	☐	☐	☐	_____
reading	☐	☐	☐	_____

Useful Language

Questions
- What is your hobby?
- How often do you . . . ?
- How long have you . . . ?

Answers
- I like . . .
- I usually . . . once a week.
- I've been -ing for . . . years.

Details
- Free time activities: reading / watching movies / camping / playing the piano / gardening / collecting trading cards / traveling
- Frequency: always / often / regularly / sometimes / occasionally / rarely / never

---

Notes

I usually play tennis once a week.

頻度を説明するとき、「1週間に○回」というのは a week の前に回数を表す語 (once, twice, three times など) を示します。月のときは "about twice a month" のように表します。「毎週末」は "every weekend"、「ほぼ毎週末」は "most weekends" を使います。

III Conversation 8

Part 1: Listen to the conversation and choose the most appropriate answer (a~d) for each question.

Get the gist

1. What are John and Nozomi going to do?
   a. They are going to go to a concert.
   b. They are going to go to a party.
   c. They are going to go to a baseball game.
   d. They are going to go to karaoke.

2. Who are John and Nozomi most likely?
   a. Classmates
   b. Co-workers
   c. Teacher and student
   d. Brother and sister

Get the details

1. What do John and Nozomi both like?
   a. Playing guitar
   b. Music
   c. Sports
   d. Games

2. What sport does Nozomi like watching?
   a. Cricket
   b. Soccer
   c. Football
   d. Baseball

3. What is Nozomi's favorite activity?
   a. Dancing
   b. Playing games
   c. Singing
   d. Playing piano

4. What does John probably want to do?
   a. Play computer games
   b. Play the guitar
   c. Learn to dance
   d. Learn to sing

Part 2: Listen to the conversation again and write the missing words or phrases in the spaces.

John: Hey Nozomi, we're going to karaoke after class. If you're (1) _____, why don't you come with us?

Nozomi: Thanks, John. I'd (2) _____ _____ _____. I didn't know you liked singing.

John: I'm not a very good singer, but I love music. I (3) _____ play the guitar in my free time. What are you into?

Nozomi: Well, I like music, too. I can play the piano a little. But my favorite pastime is playing games on my computer or phone.

John: Really? Actually, I'm a big sports fan, so I (4) _____ playing sports like football or cricket. Do you do any sports, Nozomi?

Nozomi: No, I don't play any sports. But I like watching baseball games on TV occasionally, and I love dancing. I'm (5) _____ _____ _____ the Dance Club.

John: Oh, I didn't know that you'd joined the Dance Club. I love music, but I'm a terrible dancer.

Nozomi: I'd (6) _____ _____ _____ teach you to dance.

John: That sounds (7) _____. Shall we go dancing after we go to karaoke?

Nozomi: That's a great idea. Now let's eat. I think I'll have the lunch set.

Speaking Practice: Practice the conversation with your partner.

IV ⎪Pronunciation Check

短縮形

日常会話では apostrophe（アポストロフィ）を使って表現される短縮形がよく使われます。例えば、「ぜひ〜したい」という意味の "I would love to . . ." は "I'd love to . . ." となります。I had, would の短縮形はいずれも I'd で、発音も同じ【ɑɪd】です。どの語が短縮されているかは文脈から判断するようにしましょう。

Exercises

 9

▪ Look at the sentences below and circle the ones you hear. Then, practice saying the sentences, paying attention to contractions.

1. I would like to join the tennis club. / I'd like to join the tennis club.

2. I will tell you the results soon. / I'll tell you the results soon.

3. I had been working as an accountant for ten years. / I'd been working as an accountant for ten years.

V ⎪Focus on Function

That sounds fantastic.「素晴らしいね」

会話のなかで、肯定的な感想を述べたいときに使える表現です。fantastic 以外にも interesting, good, great, fun などの語を使って、自分の意見を伝えてみましょう。非常にカジュアルな言い方で、that を省略して "Sounds fantastic!" と言うこともできます。
例）A: I'm planning to have a picnic this weekend.（週末にピクニックをしようと思うんだ）
　　B: That sounds fun!（それは楽しそうだね！）
また、"That sounds. . ." のフレーズは、"That sounds awful"（それはひどい）のようにネガティブな感想を述べるときにも使えます。

Exercises

▪ Look at the sentences below and write a reply using *That sounds*.

1. **A:** The new coach has amazing skills and is a great teacher.
   B: _____

2. **A:** There are many students in my class from other countries.
   B: _____

3. **A:** I'm a member of the football club. Our team won the championship.
   B: _____

VI | Find out

In the conversation on p.10, Nozomi described her favorite free time activities to John. Think about one of your interests. Then, write the questions below. Next, write your answers to the questions. Finally, ask a partner the questions and find out what their interest is.

Your interest: _____

Q1: (When / do / do) _____?

You: _____ | Your partner: _____

Q2: (How / often / do) _____?

You: _____ | Your partner: _____

Q3: (Are / member / club) _____?

You: _____ | Your partner: _____

Q4: (When / did / start) _____?

You: _____ | Your partner: _____

Q5: Your question: _____?

You: _____ | Your partner: _____

Your partner's interest: _____

Useful Language

Noun phrases: art / sport / dance / food / crafts / music / education
Verb phrases: paint / draw / ride / cook / sew / knit / listen / make / play / travel
Adjectives: interesting / healthy / exciting / classical / traditional / modern

《好きなものを話してみよう》

趣味について話すとき、"My hobby is . . ." という表現でも良いのですが、"I like . . ." や "I'm interested in . . ." も使ってみましょう。また "I'm into . . ." で夢中になっていることを表すこともできます。

例）I'm really into K-pop now.（最近すっかり K ポップにはまっているの）

UNIT

3

Who're they?
– Talking about Friends and Family

I Vocabulary

Part 1: Match the words and phrases (a~j) with their meanings (1~10).

a. younger	b. wife	c. parents	d. only child	e. take after
f. colleague	g. mutual	h. classmate	i. niece	j. nephew

1. _____ a person with no brothers or sisters
2. _____ a person in the same class or on the same course
3. _____ the son of a brother or sister
4. _____ the daughter of a brother or sister
5. _____ a co-worker
6. _____ to resemble, to be like
7. _____ not as old as, inferior in age
8. _____ shared, similar
9. _____ a female partner in a marriage
10. _____ mother and father, a child's caregivers

Part 2: Complete the dialogs with words and phrases from Part 1.

1. **A:** That's a nice picture. Who're they?
   B: That's my older brother. He's a doctor. That's my _____ sister. She's only seven.
2. **A:** Who in your family do you _____?
   B: I'd have to say my father. People say we have similar eyes.
3. **A:** Who's that with your brother? Is that his daughter?
   B: Yes, that's my _____, Aniqa. She's cute, isn't she?
4. **A:** Who are you going to the concert with?
   B: None of my friends or family want to go, so I'm going with a(n) _____. We've worked together for years and both like the same kind of music.
5. **A:** Why is Ray your best friend?
   B: We have a lot of _____ interests. We both like chess, judo, and cars. We really have a lot in common.

II │ Warm-up for Listening & Speaking

■ **Listening Practice:** Listen to two people talking about their families and friends. Write the speakers' names and check (✔) the correct boxes.

1. Name: _____

	Yes	No
has a big family	☐	☐
has a lot of friends	☐	☐
sees their friends often	☐	☐
has a pet	☐	☐

2. Name: _____

	Yes	No
has a big family	☐	☐
has a lot of friends	☐	☐
sees their friends often	☐	☐
has a pet	☐	☐

■ **Speaking Practice:** How much do you know about your family and friends? Check the boxes below and talk to your partner about their family and friends.

	A lot	Some / A bit	Little / Nothing	Reason
your family's work	☐	☐	☐	_____
your family's hobbies	☐	☐	☐	_____
your family's friends	☐	☐	☐	_____
your friends' work	☐	☐	☐	_____
your friends' families	☐	☐	☐	_____

Useful Language

Questions
- What does your father/mother do?
- Do you know what your family's hobbies are?
- How many people are there in your family?

Answers
- My . . . is a . . .
- My . . . likes . . .
- There are . . . people in my family.

Details
- People: younger brother / older sister / parents / cousin / uncle / aunt / nephew / niece / wife / father-in-law / stepsister / ex-husband / only child

Notes

兄弟や子供、配偶者のことを話すとき、"My husband, John, is . . ." のように最初に名前を示して、それ以降は会話の中で "my husband" ではなく個人名で表現するのが自然です。ただ、両親については日本と同じように "my mother" や "my mom" を使います。

III Conversation

 12

Part 1: Listen to the conversation and choose the most appropriate answer (a~d) for each question.

Get the gist

1. Where are Sam and Kana most likely?
   a. In a shop   **b.** In a restaurant
   c. At university   **d.** At home

2. Who is Kana most likely?
   a. Sam's sister   **b.** Sam's teacher
   c. Sam's classmate   **d.** Sam's girlfriend

Get the details

1. What did Kana find it hard to do?
   a. Think of ideas for the homework
   b. Know which idea to start with for the homework
   c. Ask Sam the homework question
   d. Give her family and friends advice

2. Who does Sam think gives the best advice?
   a. Kana   **b.** It depends on the situation
   c. Only his friends   **d.** Only his family

3. What topic does Sam ask his family for advice on?
   a. His girlfriend   **b.** His homework
   c. His work   **d.** The things he likes

4. Why does Kana think Sam is lucky?
   a. Because he has a girlfriend.
   b. Because his family has experience with issues.
   c. Because he makes sense.
   d. Because he can talk to lots of people about his problems.

Part 2: Listen to the conversation again and write the missing words or phrases in the spaces.

Sam: OK, Kana, now class is over let's (1) _____ _____ _____ _____ we have to do for our homework for our Discussion class. It's a tough one this week.

Kana: I know, Sam. I looked at it a little bit last night and I found it hard to come up with any ideas.

Sam: Really? I'm the (2) _____. I have too many things to say about it! My problem is I don't know which idea to start with.

Kana: OK, well, I guess the best place to start is with the actual question we were given. So, "Who do you think gives you better advice, friends or family?"

Sam: Well, I really think it depends on the situation. If I want (3) _____ _____ _____ _____ about my girlfriend or homework or school life, then I ask my friends because they understand my situation better.

Kana: Alright, that (4) _____ sense. So, when do you ask your family for advice?

Sam: I talk to them when it comes to money or work or things like that. They have more experience with (5) _____ issues.

Kana: Wow. You're lucky to have so many people (6) _____ _____ _____ about your problems. I don't really feel comfortable talking to people about things like that. I find it hard to open up.

Sam: You shouldn't be embarrassed to ask for advice — (7) _____ needs help sometimes. Look, next time you have a problem you can always tell me.

Kana: Thanks. Well, now you mention it . . .

Speaking Practice: Practice the conversation with your partner.

IV Pronunciation Check

リダクション：消える音 t

Reduction（リダクション）という音が消える現象を理解することで、英語のリスニング力や発音が格段に上達します。スペルに表記されていても、実際には聞こえない音がいくつかあり、覚えている単語と聞こえる単語が一致しない場合があるので注意が必要です。ここでは t の音を意識して発音してみましょう。

例）last night → las(t) nigh(t) のように聞こえます。

Exercises

 13

Listen to the recording and choose the sentence which uses reduction, A or B. Then, practice saying the sentences, paying attention to reduction.

1. I want some strong, hot coffee.   A   B

2. Amy passed the bar exam on her first attempt.   A   B

3. One of the great things about this machine is its light weight.   A   B

V Focus on Function

Alright. 相手に応答する

相手の話していることに対して、上手に応答できるとスムーズに会話が進みます。"Alright" は、"All right" のカジュアルな表現で、「わかったよ」と同意や容認を表します。多くの場合、フォーマルな文章では "All right" を使うようです。理解したことを示す表現としては、他に OK. / I see. / Right. / I understand. などがあります。

驚きを示す "Really?" "Are you sure?" なども覚えておくと便利です。

Exercises

Look at the sentences below and write a reply.

1. **A:** I started living by myself this year.
   B: _____

2. **A:** It is more important to spend time with friends than family.
   B: _____

3. **A:** I'm looking for a larger apartment so I can get a cat.
   B: _____

VI ┃ Find out

In the conversation on p.16, Sam and Kana were talking about asking friends and family for advice. Think about some questions you can ask your classmates about talking to their friends and family and write them below. Then, write your answers to the questions. Finally, ask a partner the questions and find out about them.

Q1: (Who / talk to / more / friends or family) _____?	
You: _____	Your partner: _____
Q2: (What / like / talk to / friends / about) _____?	
You: _____	Your partner: _____
Q3: (Do / often / chat online / friends) _____?	
You: _____	Your partner: _____
Q4: (What / talk / family / about) _____?	
You: _____	Your partner: _____
Q5: (Who / ask / advice) _____?	
You: _____	Your partner: _____
Q6: Your question: _____?	
You: _____	Your partner: _____

Useful Language

Noun phrases: part-time job / club activity / interpersonal relationship / colleague / job hunting

Verb phrases: study / ask for advice / worry about / decide / change one's opinion / take after

Adjectives: reliable / careful / mature / intelligent / easy / comfortable / mutual

《人間関係について話してみよう》
日本語の「人間関係」を英語にすると、例えば次のような表現があります。
interpersonal relationship / person-to-person relationship / human relation
「友人関係」は "friendship"、「恋愛関係」は "romantic relationship" です。「〜との関係」と言うときは、"relationship with . . ." を使いましょう。

What shall we watch?
– Talking about Movies and TV

I Vocabulary

Part 1: Match the words (a~j) with their meanings (1~10).

a. scene	b. famous	c. actor	d. fantasy	e. crime
f. romance	g. horror	h. comedy	i. soundtrack	j. action

1. _____ a person who performs or stars in a play, movie, or TV show, etc.
2. _____ events that happen quickly and that cause feelings of danger and excitement
3. _____ a story that is meant to make people laugh
4. _____ a story that is meant to make people feel scared
5. _____ activity that is against the law
6. _____ a part of a story in which a particular activity happens
7. _____ a story about things that happen in an imaginary world
8. _____ the sounds and especially the music recorded for a movie
9. _____ known or recognized by many people
10. _____ a love story

Part 2: Complete the dialogs with words from Part 1.

1. **A:** That was a great movie, wasn't it?
   B: Yes, it was. It was so exciting. The _____ at the end when they kissed was so romantic.
2. **A:** What are you listening to?
   B: The _____ to that sports movie we saw last week. I really liked the music, so I downloaded it.
3. **A:** What kind of TV shows and movies do you like?
   B: I love _____. I wish I could use magic and fight dragons.
4. **A:** Oh no. Not him. I can't stand that guy.
   B: Why not?
   A: He thinks he's _____ because he was on TV once. Once!
5. **A:** What is this TV show about?
   B: It's a crime _____. If you watch it, you won't be able to stop laughing.

II Warm-up for Listening & Speaking

Listening Practice: Listen to two people talking about movies they watched. Write the movie genres each person liked the best and check (✔) the correct boxes.

1. The genre Jil liked best: _____

	Yes	No
bought snacks	☐	☐
watched a horror movie	☐	☐
liked the romance movie	☐	☐
enjoyed the comedy	☐	☐

2. The genre Colin liked best: _____

	Yes	No
bought snacks	☐	☐
watched a horror movie	☐	☐
liked the romance movie	☐	☐
enjoyed the comedy	☐	☐

Speaking Practice: What is important to you when you choose a movie or TV show to watch? Check the boxes below and talk to your partner about the movies and TV shows they like.

	Very important	Quite important	Not important	Reason
exciting action scenes	☐	☐	☐	_____
romance	☐	☐	☐	_____
funny	☐	☐	☐	_____
famous actor or actress	☐	☐	☐	_____
good soundtrack	☐	☐	☐	_____

Useful Language

Questions
- What kind of . . . do you like?
- How often do you watch . . . ?
- Why do you like . . . movies/TV shows?

Answers
- I like . . . movies because . . .
- I usually watch . . . once a month.

Details
- Genres: comedy / action / horror / mystery / drama / romance / science fiction / fantasy / historical drama / documentary / biography

Notes

I watch a TV comedy sometimes.

「時々」と言う場合、どのような語を思い浮かべますか？ sometimes はよく使われる単語ですが、occasionally, at times, now and then などの言い方もあります。「めったにない／まれな」と言う場合は、rarely を使いましょう。

III ║Conversation

 16

■ **Part 1:** Listen to the conversation and choose the most appropriate answer (a~d) for each question.

▌ *Get the gist*

1. What are Colin and Jil talking about?
   a. Taking a trip together   **b.** Jil's job as a detective
   c. The cold weather   **d.** Things that they like

2. What will Jil likely do tomorrow?
   a. Watch TV with Colin   **b.** Watch a comedy show
   c. See a movie one more time   **d.** Watch a crime drama again

▌ *Get the details*

1. What kind of TV show does Colin like best?
   a. Crime drama   **b.** Science fiction
   c. Comedy   **d.** Horror

2. What kind of TV show do Colin and Jil both like?
   a. Crime drama   **b.** Science fiction
   c. Comedy   **d.** Horror

3. What kind of movie doesn't Colin like?
   a. Crime drama   **b.** Science fiction
   c. Comedy   **d.** Horror

4. What did Colin think about the movie?
   a. It was scary.   **b.** It was exciting.
   c. It was funny.   **d.** It was cool.

Part 2: Listen to the conversation again and write the missing words or phrases in the spaces.

Colin: Did you (1) _____ *Legend of the Galactic Traveller* last night, Jil?

Jil: No, I didn't. Is it a science fiction show? They're your favorite, aren't they, Colin?

Colin: That's right. I (2) _____ _____ _____ didn't see it. It was so exciting!

Jil: Well, I don't really like science fiction. I (3) _____ crime dramas, like *Genius Detective Miwa*.

Colin: Oh, I like that, too. The action (4) _____ are so cool, and the actor who plays Miwa is really cute. (5)_____ _____ _____ her movie?

Jil: You mean *The Curse of the Giant Kitten*? Yes, I saw it last week. It's so funny. I couldn't stop laughing.

Colin: Is it a comedy? I (6) _____ it was a horror movie. That's why I haven't seen it. I don't like horror movies.

Jil: It's a comedy horror movie, so it's not really scary. You should definitely go and see it.

Colin: Okay, I will. It's a shame that you've already seen it, though. I was hoping we could go together.

Jil: I (7) _____ _____ _____ it again. Why don't we go tomorrow?

Speaking Practice: Practice the conversation with your partner.

IV ‖Pronunciation Check

【si:】 と 【ʃi:】 の発音

英語では、綴りが違うけれども同じ発音や、似ているけれども違う発音の単語があります。seen と scene は、品詞も意味も異なりますが、両方とも同じ発音【si:n】です。【si:】と【ʃi:】の発音は似ているようで違うので、注意する必要があります。【si:】は口を横に広げて「ス」と「シ」の間くらいの音で、【ʃi:】は口をそれほど横に拡げません。人称代名詞の she は【ʃi:】と発音します。
これらの単語を使った有名な早口言葉があります。
　She sells seashells by the seashore. (彼女は海岸で貝殻を売っている)
日本人には違いが難しい発音ですが、意識して練習してみましょう。

▌*Exercises* ╱

 17

▌Look at the sentences below and circle the pronunciations that you hear. Then, practice saying the sentences, paying attention to the sounds /ʃiː/ and /siː/.

1. I look forward to <u>seeing</u> you.　　　　　　A /ʃiː/　　B /siː/

2. There are many <u>sheep</u> and goats on the farm.　　A /ʃiː/　　B /siː/

3. Sitting in his <u>seat</u>, Ken fills in an order <u>sheet</u>.

　　　　A /ʃiː/　B /siː/　　　　　A /ʃiː/　B /siː/

V ‖Focus on Function

I don't mind . . . 「～しても構いませんよ」

動詞の mind は「嫌だと思う」という意味ですが、会話では否定文で「～しても構わない、気にしない」の意味で使われることがよくあります。mind の後ろには名詞句や動名詞 (-ing) が続くので覚えておきましょう。
例) I don't mind seeing the movie again. (その映画をもう一度見ても構わないよ)
　　I don't mind what they say. (彼らが言っていることなんて、気にしないよ)

▌*Exercises* ╱

▌Complete the sentences below using *don't mind.*

1. 忙しそうだね。手伝うよ。
　 You look busy. I ＿＿＿＿＿＿ ＿＿＿＿＿＿ ＿＿＿＿＿＿ you.

2. 僕たちは天気なんて気にしないよ。
　 We ＿＿＿＿＿＿ ＿＿＿＿＿＿ ＿＿＿＿＿＿ ＿＿＿＿＿＿ .

3. 君が疲れているのなら、彼女は運転しても構わないと言った。
　 She said she ＿＿＿＿＿＿ ＿＿＿＿＿＿ ＿＿＿＿＿＿ if you are tired.

VI | Find out

In the conversation on p.22, Colin and Jil talked about movies and TV shows. Think about your favorite movie or TV show. Then, write the questions below. Next, write your answers to the questions. Finally, ask a partner the questions and find out what their favorite movie or TV show is.

Your favorite movie or TV show: _____	
Q1: (Is / movie / TV show) _____?	
You: _____	Your partner: _____
Q2: (What / kind) _____?	
You: _____	Your partner: _____
Q3: (Why / like) _____?	
You: _____	Your partner: _____
Q4: (Who / leading role) _____?	
You: _____	Your partner: _____
Q5: Your question: _____?	
You: _____	Your partner: _____
Your partner's favorite kind of movie or TV show: _____	

Useful Language

Noun phrases: actor / actress / director / leading role / supporting actor / hero / heroine / villain
Verb phrases: The . . . movie is . . . / The . . . scene(s) is (are) . . . / XX appear(s) as . . .
Adjectives: scary / funny / cool / amazing / heartwarming / touching / boring

《出演者について話してみよう》
テレビや映画の出演者が「〜役で出演している」と言うには、appear as . . . を使います。「主役を務める」と言うときは、play the leading role (part) と表現できます。
例）Robert Downey, Jr. appears as Sherlock Holmes.
　　Emma Watson plays the leading role in *Beauty and the Beast*.

UNIT 5

What are you listening to?
– Talking about Music

I Vocabulary

Part 1: Match the words (a~j) with their meanings (1~10).

a. instrument   b. live   c. solo   d. moving   e. perform

f. musical   g. performance   h. band   i. orchestra   j. concert

1. _____ to entertain an audience by singing, acting, etc.
2. _____ a small group of musicians who play music together
3. _____ done in front of an audience, not a recording
4. _____ having a strong emotional effect
5. _____ relating to music
6. _____ performed by one singer or musician
7. _____ an activity that a person or group does to entertain an audience
8. _____ a group of musicians who play music together and who are led by a conductor
9. _____ a device that is used to make music
10. _____ a public performance of music

Part 2: Complete the dialogs with words from Part 1.

1. **A:** What's your favorite piece of classical music?
   B: It's Albinoni's Adagio. It's a really _____ piece of music. Whenever I listen to it, I start to cry.

2. **A:** My dream is to perform a solo _____ at Tokyo Dome.
   B: Really? Then you need to do a lot more singing practice. Going to karaoke once a week isn't enough.

3. **A:** You can play the guitar, can't you? So how about . . .
   B: Don't ask. I'm not going to join your rock _____. I don't like that kind of music.

4. **A:** Wow, she is an amazing piano player.
   B: I know. Did you know that this is her first public _____? I think she's going to be really famous.

5. **A:** What do you want to do on the first day of the culture festival?
   B: I really want to see the school _____ perform Tchaikovsky's 1812 Overture.

II Warm-up for Listening & Speaking

 18, 19

Listening Practice: Listen to two people talking about music. Write the musical club activities they do and check (✔) the correct boxes.

1. Musical club activity: _____	Yes	No
watch music videos	☐	☐
dance	☐	☐
sing	☐	☐
play the violin	☐	☐

2. Musical club activity: _____	Yes	No
watch music videos	☐	☐
dance	☐	☐
sing	☐	☐
play the violin	☐	☐

Speaking Practice: What kind of musical activities are important to you? Check the boxes below and talk to your partner about the musical activities they like.

	Very important	Quite important	Not important	Reason
listening to music	☐	☐	☐	_____
watching music videos	☐	☐	☐	_____
singing	☐	☐	☐	_____
dancing	☐	☐	☐	_____
going to concerts	☐	☐	☐	_____

Useful Language

Questions
- What kind of music do you like?
- Can you play . . . ?
- Who is your favorite . . . ?

Answers
- I like . . .
- I can play . . .
- XX is my favorite . . .

Details
- Music: rock / jazz / country / hip hop / blues / folk / R&B / dance / soul / reggae
- Performances: gig / [live] concert / solo / recital
- Groups: solo artist / duet / trio / quartet / quintet / band / orchestra

Notes

She can play the piano.
「〜を演奏する」と言う場合、基本的に楽器には定冠詞 the を付けます。ただし、「楽器を買う、作る」などのときは the を付ける必要はないので区別しましょう。
例) He bought a guitar yesterday.
　　My father makes violins.
また、日本語の「クラシック音楽」は classical music で、classic は「最高級の、第一級の」という意味です。

III ‖Conversation

 20

Part 1: Listen to the conversation and choose the most appropriate answer (a~d) for each question.

Get the gist

1. What are Wendy and Jon talking about?
    a. Their weekend plans
    b. Wendy's hobby
    c. Jon's favorite kinds of music
    d. Their summer vacation plans

2. What is true about Wendy and Jon?
    a. Wendy likes music more than Jon.
    b. Jon likes music more than Wendy.
    c. They both like music.
    d. Neither of them likes music.

Get the details

1. What didn't Wendy know about Jon?
    a. He could sing.
    b. He played the piano.
    c. He liked rock.
    d. He played the bass guitar.

2. What do Wendy and Jon both like?
    a. Kyoto
    b. Rock
    c. Singing
    d. Playing the piano

3. Where do Wendy and Jon both go?
    a. To junior high school
    b. To senior high school
    c. To university
    d. To the Fuji Rock Festival

4. What does Jon probably want Wendy to do?
    a. Join his band
    b. Watch his band
    c. Go to the Fuji Rock Festival
    d. Play rock music together

Part 2: Listen to the conversation again and write the missing words or phrases in the spaces.

Wendy: What are you doing on the (1) _____, Jon?

Jon: I'm going to Kyoto. My band is playing (2) _____ _____ _____ there tomorrow.

Wendy: Wow! That's so cool. Are you the (3) _____?

Jon: No, I'm not. I play the bass guitar.

Wendy: Really? I didn't know you could play (4) _____ _____ _____. Have you been playing long?

Jon: Yes, I've been playing the bass guitar (5) _____ I was in junior high school, and I started my band when I was at university.

Wendy: That's great. I started playing the trumpet in my junior high school orchestra club, but I stopped after (6) _____ _____ _____. What kind of music does your band play?

Jon: We're a rock band. Do you like rock, Wendy?

Wendy: Yes, I do. I love it! I go to the Fuji Rock Festival every (7) _____.

Jon: Me, too! So, would you like to come to my concert tomorrow?

Wendy: Sure. I don't have any other plans.

Speaking Practice: Practice the conversation with your partner.

IV Pronunciation Check

ＬとＲの発音

英語のＬとＲの発音は、多くの日本人が苦手とするものです。特にカタカナ表記で発音を覚えてしまうと区別が難しくなるので、注意しましょう。Ｒは巻き舌で発音する必要はありません。
Ｌの発音：舌を上向きにして、上の歯の根元に付けるように発音する。
Ｒの発音：口の中のどこにも舌先を付けずに、口の奥のほうで発音する。
リスニングの際にＬの音は比較的はっきりと聞こえます。Ｒの音は口を「ウ」の形にしてすぼめてから発音するようなイメージです。

Exercises

 21

🔲 Look at the sentences below and circle the words that you hear. Then, practice saying the sentences, paying attention to the sounds /l/ and /r/.

1. Turn (**light / right**) at the next traffic (**light / right**).

2. The scholar pointed out that the declining birth (**late / rate**) is caused by (**late / rate**) marriage.

3. I purchased this (**flying / frying**) pan at a (**flea / free**) market.

V Focus on Function

Since I was in high school . . .「高校生のときから〜」

「〜以来、〜から」と過去のある時点から別の時点まで継続していることを示すとき、since を使って表現します。"I have played the piano since I was five years old." のように、完了形を伴って使うことが多いのですが、"It is ten years since I left school." と現在形や過去形と共に使う場合もあります。when「〜のときに」との違いに注意しましょう。since の後ろには、主語＋動詞あるいは名詞のみを続けて状況を示します。
例）I have known Joe since I was a child.（ジョーは子供のときから知っています）

Exercises

🔲 Look at the sentences below and circle the correct words.

1. We have been working together (**when / since**) this company was founded.

2. Cathy was watching TV (**when / since**) he arrived.

3. I have not seen Nick (**when / since**) Wednesday.

VI | Find out

In the conversation on p.28, Wendy and Jon talked about music. Think about your favorite music artist. Then, write the questions below. Next, write your answers to the questions. Finally, ask a partner the questions and find out who their favorite music artist is.

Your favorite music artist: _____	
Q1: (Is / singer / group) _____ ?	
You: _____	Your partner: _____
Q2: (What / kind / music) _____ ?	
You: _____	Your partner: _____
Q3: (Do / appear / TV) _____ ?	
You: _____	Your partner: _____
Q4: (Have / been / concert) _____ ?	
You: _____	Your partner: _____
Q5: Your question: _____ ?	
You: _____	Your partner: _____
Your partner's favorite music artist: _____	

Useful Language

Noun phrases: solo / chorus / tempo / rhythm / musical note / beat / melody
Verb phrases: attend a concert / give (hold) a concert / form a trio / tap a rhythm / perform
Adjectives: fast / slow / brisk / sedate / restful / exciting / bouncing / moving

《音楽について話してみよう》
好きなリズムやテンポはありますか？　例えば、「速いテンポで演奏する」は "play (the piece) at a fast tempo" と表現します。piece は楽曲など作品を意味します。他にも、"I like the intense rhythm of a rock song."（ロックの激しいリズムが好きなんだ）など形容詞を使って説明してみましょう。

UNIT 6

What are you reading?
– Talking about Books

I │ Vocabulary

Part 1: Match the words (a~j) with their meanings (1~10).

a. cover	b. character	c. author / writer	d. recommend	e. fascinating
f. translate	g. novel	h. fiction	i. nonfiction	j. biography

1. _____ a person who has written something
2. _____ writing that is about facts or real events
3. _____ a person who appears in a story, book, play, movie, or TV show
4. _____ to suggest, to advise
5. _____ a long, written story usually about imaginary characters and events
6. _____ the outer part of a book or magazine
7. _____ the story of a real person's life written by a different person
8. _____ to change words from one language into another
9. _____ very interesting or appealing
10. _____ stories which are imagined by the writer

Part 2: Complete the dialogs with words from Part 1.

1. **A:** This book is _____. I can't put it down.
   B: Really? What's it about?

2. **A:** I love reading true stories about peoples' lives.
   B: Really? I prefer reading _____. I find it a lot more relaxing.

3. **A:** Who's your favorite _____, Selena?
   B: Probably Haruki Murakami. I love his books.

4. **A:** What Japanese _____ do you recommend?
   B: I think you would like *I Am A Cat* by Soseki Natsume. It's famous all over the world.

5. **A:** What are you reading?
   B: It's a(n) _____ about my favorite actor. He has had a very interesting life so far.

Listening Practice: Listen to two people talking about things they have read recently. Write what the speakers read and check (✔) the correct boxes.

1. Read: _____

	Yes	No
was interesting	☐	☐
was difficult	☐	☐
was well-written	☐	☐
would recommend	☐	☐

2. Read: _____

	Yes	No
was interesting	☐	☐
was difficult	☐	☐
was well-written	☐	☐
would recommend	☐	☐

Speaking Practice: What do you think is important when you read a book? Check the boxes below and talk to your partner about reading.

	Very important	Quite important	Not important	Reason
the length	☐	☐	☐	_____
the front cover	☐	☐	☐	_____
the characters	☐	☐	☐	_____
the story	☐	☐	☐	_____
the difficulty	☐	☐	☐	_____

Useful Language

Questions
- How often do you read . . . ?
- What is the . . . book you have ever read?
- How important do you think . . . is/are?
- Why do you think . . . is/are . . . ?

Answers
- I (don't) think . . . is/are . . . because . . .
- In my opinion, . . . is/are . . . because . . .

Details
- Adjectives: boring / interesting / attractive / cool / believable / realistic / complicated / easy

Notes
How important do you think . . . ?
「どれくらい」など程度を尋ねるときには、how +形容詞（副詞）を使います。また、interesting や amusing（面白い）といった形容詞を覚えておくと、具体的な説明ができるようになります。

III ‖Conversation

 24

🔹 **Part 1:** Listen to the conversation and choose the most appropriate answer (a~d) for each question.

Get the gist

1. Who are Ron and Tina most likely?

    a. Teacher and student   **b.** Friends

    c. Co-workers   **d.** Bookshop staffer and customer

2. What are they mainly talking about?

    a. Tina's homework   **b.** Learning another language

    c. Their favorite books   **d.** Ron's part-time job

Get the details

1. What kind of text is Tina reading?

    a. Biography   **b.** A comic

    c. Romance   **d.** Science fiction

2. What kind of books does Ron like to read?

    a. Science fiction and biographies   **b.** Biographies and romance fiction

    c. Science fiction and romance fiction **d.** Comics and romance fiction

3. Who is Tina's favorite author?

    a. Kyoichi Katayama   **b.** Ruth Cardello

    c. Maid for the Billionaire   **d.** Legacy series

4. How many books are in the Legacy series?

    a. 1   **b.** 2

    c. 5   **d.** 7

Part 2: Listen to the conversation again and write the missing words or phrases in the spaces.

Ron: Hi, Tina. What are you reading?

Tina: Oh, hi Ron. It's an article about a famous English author. I need to read it for my next class. The teacher is going to ask us (1) _____ about it.

Ron: Wow, that sounds (2) _____ . Is it difficult?

Tina: It is a bit, yes. I'm not (3) _____ _____ reading biographies. Normally, I just read comics or romance novels and they are very (4) _____ !

Ron: Oh, I prefer science fiction, but I like romance fiction, too. Who's your favorite author?

Tina: Someone called Ruth Cardello. Have you (5) _____ _____ her?

Ron: Sorry, no. Maybe I have heard of one of her books, though. Which is the most (6) _____ ?

Tina: Maybe a book called *Maid for the Billionaire*. It's the first book in the Legacy series. There are seven books in total.

Ron: Seven? Gee, it would take me a long time to read that many books. Especially in English. Now that I'm studying and working part-time, I don't get much time to read just for fun.

Tina: I know. Me, too. I (7) _____ _____ _____ read more. So, are there any Japanese books that you could recommend for me?

Ron: You should try a book by Kyoichi Katayama called *Crying Out Love, In The Center of the World*. It is a best-seller and has been translated into English. It's sad, but very romantic.

Tina: That sounds fascinating. I want to read it. Thanks for the recommendation!

Speaking Practice: Practice the conversation with your partner.

IV Pronunciation Check

似ている音に注意しよう

Unit 5 では L と R の発音について学びました。その他にも英語には似ている発音の単語があります。今回の会話に出てくる heard【həːrd】は hard【háːrd】と間違いやすい単語です。以下の例のように、聞き分けるのが難しいものがいくつかあるので、チェックしておきましょう。正しい発音を覚えるのと同時に、会話の内容から判断できるようになることも大切です。

例）seat / sheet　　bath / bus　　debt / dead

Exercises

 25

🔲 **Look at the sentences below and circle the words you hear. Then, practice saying the sentences, paying attention to the pronunciations.**

1. This (**desert / dessert**) plant was cooked as a (**desert / dessert**).

2. I (**think / sink**) that the wall is slowly (**thinking / sinking**).

3. He was a (**first / fast**) runner, and came in (**first / fast**).

V Focus on Function

I wish I could . . . 「〜できれば良いのに」

実際には難しいけれども、できれば良いのに、という気持ちを伝える表現です。can の過去形 could を使いますが、過去を示しているわけではありません。依頼や誘いを断らなくてはならないときにも便利なフレーズです。"I wish I could . . . , but . . ."「〜できれば良いんだけど、〜なんだ」のように、but の次にできない理由をつなげると、会話がスムーズに続きます。

例）I wish I could go with you, but I have a meeting today.
　　（君と一緒に行ければ良いんだけど、今日は会議があるんだ）

Exercises

🔲 **Look at the sentences below and write a reply using *I wish I could*.**

1. **A:** I don't get much time to sleep nowadays because I'm busy with studying and working.
   B: I know. Me, too. _____

2. **A:** We're having a party on Saturday. Would you like to come?
   B: _____

3. **A:** I saw a turtle while swimming in the sea.
   B: Really? _____

VI │ Find out

In the conversation on p.34, Ron described a book by Kyoichi Katayama. Think about a popular book you like. Then, write the questions below. Next, write your answers to the questions. Finally, ask a partner the questions and find out what the book they like is.

The book you like: _____	
Q1: (What / genre) _____?	
You: _____	Your partner: _____
Q2: (Who / author) _____?	
You: _____	Your partner: _____
Q3: (Has / movie or TV series / based on the book) _____?	
You: _____	Your partner: _____
Q4: (Why / like) _____?	
You: _____	Your partner: _____
Q5: Your question: _____?	
You: _____	Your partner: _____
The book your partner likes: _____	

Useful Language

Noun phrases: romance / science fiction / nonfiction / horror / crime / fantasy / literary novel / short story

Verb phrases: It was written by . . . / It was written in . . . / It has been translated into . . . / It has been made into a . . . / The TV series stars . . .

Adjectives: romantic / exciting / terrifying / thrilling / amazing / emotional / moving

《好きな本を紹介してみよう》

本には様々なジャンルがありますね。他にもどのような種類があるか考えてみましょう。誰によって書かれたかは by、何語で書かれたかは in など、前置詞が異なるので注意が必要です。小説が映画化された場合は、The novel has been made into a movie. という表現を使います。また、誰が主演しているか説明するときには star（動詞で「～を主演させる」という意味）を使います。

例）The TV series stars Adam Driver.（テレビシリーズではアダム・ドライバーが主演している）

UNIT 7

I'm hungry!
– Talking about Food

I Vocabulary

Part 1: Match the words (a~j) with their meanings (1~10).

a. bland	b. delicious	c. fragrant	d. disgusting	e. bitter
f. healthy	g. sweet	h. raw	i. fresh	j. spicy/hot

1. _____ a very good flavor
2. _____ a flavor that is the opposite of sweet
3. _____ a flavor associated with chili peppers and curry
4. _____ good for your body
5. _____ not cooked
6. _____ a pleasant smell
7. _____ a flavor associated with sugar
8. _____ little or no flavor
9. _____ newly made or newly gathered, not old
10. _____ a very bad flavor

Part 2: Complete the dialogs with words from Part 1.

1. **A:** What kind of food do you like best?
   B: I love _____ foods like ice cream and chocolate. How about you?

2. **A:** Are you OK, Dexter? You're sweating a lot.
   B: I know. This curry is very _____. Could I have some water, please?

3. **A:** You really like salads, don't you?
   B: Yes, I do. Doctors recommend that we eat at least five servings of _____ fruit and vegetables a day. That's why I always have salad for lunch.

4. **A:** Some people don't like the taste of *natto*, but I think it is _____.
   B: Really? I can't stand it! I think it smells bad, too.

5. **A:** The Japanese diet is well known for being very _____.
   B: Yes, and it is very tasty, too! One of my favorite Japanese foods is *tempura*!

37

II Warm-up for Listening & Speaking

 26, 27

■ **Listening Practice:** Listen to two people talking about things they have eaten or drunk recently. Write the type of food or drink and check (✔) the correct boxes.

1. Type of food or drink: _____

	Yes	No
was fragrant	☐	☐
was bland	☐	☐
was chewy	☐	☐
was spicy / hot	☐	☐

2. Type of food or drink: _____

	Yes	No
was fragrant	☐	☐
was bland	☐	☐
was bitter	☐	☐
was delicious	☐	☐

■ **Speaking Practice:** What do you think about the foods below? Check the boxes below and talk to your partner about the foods they like.

	Delicious	So so	Disgusting	Reason
natto	☐	☐	☐	_____
umeboshi	☐	☐	☐	_____
curry	☐	☐	☐	_____
pizza	☐	☐	☐	_____
fried rice	☐	☐	☐	_____

Useful Language

Questions
- What do you think about . . . ?
- Why do you think . . . is . . . ?
- What's a food you (don't) like?
- Can you cook . . . ?

Answers
- I (don't) think . . . is . . . because . . .
- From my point of view, . . . is . . . because . . .
- I (don't) like . . . because . . .

Details
- Adjectives: slimy / smelly / sour / sharp / (un)healthy / junky / oily / greasy / sweet / raw / fresh / spicy / hot / bland / bitter / salty / savory / fragrant / disgusting / cut / sliced / grated / diced / boiled / fried / baked / dried / marinated

Notes

From my point of view, . . .
「私の考えでは」と自分の意見を述べる
ときの表現です。理由を付け加えて説明
してみましょう。
その他の表現：In my opinion, . . . , My
opinion is that . . . , In my view, . . . ,
I would say that . . . ,

38

III Conversation

 28

Part 1: Listen to the conversation and choose the most appropriate answer (a~d) for each question.

Get the gist

1. Who are Max and Sakura most likely?
   - **a.** Teacher and student
   - **b.** Brother and sister
   - **c.** Classmates
   - **d.** Strangers

2. What are they mainly talking about?
   - **a.** Cooking
   - **b.** Restaurants
   - **c.** The food in Sakura's lunchbox
   - **d.** The food in Max's lunchbox

Get the details

1. What does Max say about *gyoza*?
   - **a.** He hasn't heard of them before.
   - **b.** They're really tasty.
   - **c.** They're pan-fried dumplings.
   - **d.** They go well with sauce.

2. What is in the sauce in Sakura's lunchbox?
   - **a.** Just soy sauce
   - **b.** Just vinegar
   - **c.** Just chili oil
   - **d.** Soy sauce, vinegar, and chili oil

3. How does Max feel about his lunch?
   - **a.** Happy
   - **b.** Satisfied
   - **c.** Disappointed
   - **d.** Angry

4. What will Sakura probably do in the future?
   - **a.** Make Max a lunchbox
   - **b.** Make Max a sandwich
   - **c.** Teach Max how to make a sandwich
   - **d.** Teach Max how to make a lunchbox

Part 2: Listen to the conversation again and write the missing words or phrases in the spaces.

Max: It's lunchtime at last. I skipped breakfast this morning, so I'm really hungry.

Sakura: Me, too. Let's eat.

Max: Wow, Sakura, your lunchbox looks (1) _____! What are you eating?

Sakura: Thanks, Max! These are *gyoza.* I (2) _____ _____ _____.

Max: You're such a good cook. But what are *gyoza*? I haven't (3) _____ of them before.

Sakura: I think you'd like them. They're savory pan-fried dumplings. They usually have a mixture of cabbage, meat, and garlic inside. They go really well with this spicy (4) _____.

Max: They sound really tasty. By the way, what's in the sauce?

Sakura: It's a combination of soy sauce, vinegar, and chili oil. I also have some *tamagoyaki*, that's a sweet egg roll, and some raw grated cabbage.

Max: Japanese lunchboxes always (5) _____ _____ _____. I feel a bit sad about just having a cheese sandwich now!

Sakura: Don't say that! Your sandwich looks nice, too! I love the taste of fresh bread.

Max: Thanks. But a sandwich just seems a bit bland compared to your *gyoza*. Could you (6) _____ me how to make some of the food in your lunchbox someday?

Sakura: Of course! That (7) _____ _____ _____. But only if you teach me how to make a great sandwich, too!

Speaking Practice: Practice the conversation with your partner.

IV Pronunciation Check

つながる音を聞き取ろう Part 1

単語の最後の音が子音で、次の単語が母音で始まる場合、発音が繋がって一つの語のように聞こえることがあります。次の文章の下線部を見てみましょう。

People can put a lot of different types of toppings on it.

自分でも声に出して発音し、慣れるようにしましょう。

その他の例）turn on / talk about / keep in / far away

Exercises

 29

■ Listen to the recording and mark the linking part using (‿). Then, practice saying the sentences, paying attention to linking.

1. Excuse me, I'd like to check in.

2. The meeting will be held on Tuesday.

3. He seemed to cheer up at the good news.

V Focus on Function

Could you teach me how to . . . ?

「〜の仕方を教えてくれませんか？」と頼むときの表現です。teach を tell に変えて、"Could you tell me . . . ?" と言うこともできます。道を尋ねたり、使い方を聞いたり、様々な場面で使えるフレーズです。応じるときは、"Sure." や "Of course." と答えましょう。カジュアルな言い方としては "No problem." も使えます。

Exercises

■ Translate the Japanese sentences below into English using *Could you*.

1. たこ焼きの作り方を教えてくれませんか？

   _____

2. レストランへの行き方を教えてくれませんか？（get to を使って）

   _____

3. 電子レンジ (a microwave) の使い方を教えてくれませんか？

   _____

VI | Find out

In the conversation on p.40, Sakura described some typical Japanese food to Max. Think about a type of food you like. Then, write the questions. Next, write your answers to the questions. Finally, ask a partner the questions and find out what the food they like is.

The food you like: _____	
Q1: (What / flavor / have) _____?	
You: _____	Your partner: _____
Q2: (Can / make) _____?	
You: _____	Your partner: _____
Q3: (What / ingredients) _____?	
You: _____	Your partner: _____
Q4: (How / make) _____?	
You: _____	Your partner: _____
Q5: Your question: _____?	
You: _____	Your partner: _____
The food your partner likes: _____	

Useful Language

Noun phrases: soy sauce / vineger / salt / sugar / pepper / mustard / mayonnaise
Verb phrases: fry / bake / grill / roast / boil / chop / slice / mince / mix / stir / pour / spread / add

《調理の仕方を説明しよう》
皆さんは得意料理がありますか？ 調理の手順を説明するときは、「命令形」を使います。焼く、炒める、茹でるなどの表現を覚えましょう。また、first, next など順序を伝える指示語を入れると、わかりやすくなります。
例）First, cut the cabbage. Next, mix it with the other ingredients. Then, fry thinly sliced pork . . .

UNIT 8

How do you stay fit?
– Talking about Health

I Vocabulary

Part 1: Match the words (a~j) with their meanings (1~10).

a. competitive	b. tournament	c. injury	d. exercise	e. coach
f. condition	g. strong	h. social	i. individual	j. court

1. _____ activity that requires physical effort usually done to improve or maintain health
2. _____ a person's state of health or personal fitness
3. _____ relating to an event or game with a winner or loser, wanting to win
4. _____ relating to activities in which people meet for fun and enjoyment
5. _____ an area marked out for ball games
6. _____ a group of contests between a number of teams or competitors
7. _____ a sports instructor or trainer
8. _____ having the ability to move, lift, or carry heavy weights.
9. _____ harm or damage to a person's body or feelings
10. _____ single, separate

Part 2: Complete the dialogs with words from Part 1.

1. **A:** You look _____. Do you do any sports?
   B: I don't do any sports, but I do like to exercise. I train at the local gym four times a week to stay in good condition.

2. **A:** You look tired. What's wrong?
   B: Nothing really. I've been practicing really hard for a karate _____ I have soon, though. I really want to win.

3. **A:** Do you still go running in the morning before university, Mike?
   B: No, not since I had that ankle _____. It still hurts sometimes.

4. **A:** Which do you think is more important for our health, doing _____ or eating a healthy diet?
   B: I think they're both equally important. That's why I do a lot of training and make sure I eat well.

5. **A:** Do you like the university club you joined?
   B: I do, but it's a bit too _____. Everyone wants to win every game, even at training. I thought it would be more relaxed.

🔊 **Listening Practice:** Listen to two people talking about a sport or exercise they do. Write the type of sport or exercise and check (✔) the correct boxes.

1. Sport or exercise: _____

	Yes	No
started recently	☐	☐
does it alone	☐	☐
thinks it's expensive	☐	☐
wants to continue	☐	☐

2. Sport or exercise: _____

	Yes	No
started recently	☐	☐
does it alone	☐	☐
thinks it's expensive	☐	☐
wants to continue	☐	☐

🔊 **Speaking Practice:** What do you think is important for staying healthy? Check the boxes below and talk to your partner about staying healthy.

	Very important	Quite important	Not important	Reason
eating fresh fruit	☐	☐	☐	_____
doing exercise	☐	☐	☐	_____
counting calories	☐	☐	☐	_____
sleeping well	☐	☐	☐	_____
taking supplements	☐	☐	☐	_____

Useful Language

Questions
- Do you play . . . ?
- Do you eat . . . ?
- How often do you . . . ?
- What's your favorite . . . ?

Answers
- I usually eat . . . / I play . . .
- XX is good for the health.

Details
- Health: physical condition / mental condition / muscle / flexibility / nutrient / diet

Notes

You look strong.

相手の様子や状態が「〜のようだ」と言うには、《look ＋形容詞または名詞》で表します。"excited" など過去分詞の形容詞化したものを look の後に続けて使うこともあります。

例）You look tired.（疲れているようだね）

III ‖Conversation

 32

🔲 **Part 1:** Listen to the conversation and choose the most appropriate answer (a~d) for each question.

❚ Get the gist

1. What is implied in the text?
   - **a.** They are both in good condition.
   - **b.** They are both in bad condition.
   - **c.** Jane is in better condition than Taiki.
   - **d.** Taiki is in better condition than Jane.

2. Which sport or exercise will Taiki probably do?
   - **a.** Basketball
   - **b.** Soccer
   - **c.** Cycling
   - **d.** Swimming

❚ Get the details

1. How does Taiki feel?
   - **a.** Tired
   - **b.** Sad
   - **c.** Excited
   - **d.** Bored

2. What does Jane say it is difficult to do?
   - **a.** Put on weight
   - **b.** Start exercising
   - **c.** Try different sports
   - **d.** Find something you like

3. Why doesn't Jane think Taiki would like basketball or soccer?
   - **a.** Because he prefers individual sports.
   - **b.** Because he prefers team sports.
   - **c.** Because he doesn't like the rain.
   - **d.** Because they are expensive.

4. What does Jane not say about cycling?
   - **a.** It's a great way to exercise.
   - **b.** It's a great way to get some fresh air.
   - **c.** You can go to new places doing it.
   - **d.** It's expensive.

5. What does Jane offer to do?
   - **a.** Help Taiki put on weight
   - **b.** Stop Taiki's habit of training
   - **c.** Go to the pool with Taiki
   - **d.** Teach Taiki to swim

Part 2: Listen to the conversation again and write the missing words or phrases in the spaces.

Jane: What's wrong, Taiki? **(1)** _____ _____ _____ _____ down.

Taiki: I'm not feeling great, I must admit. I've put on a lot of weight **(2)** _____. I need to start exercising again, but it's difficult.

Jane: It is difficult, but the hardest part is starting. Once you've got into the habit of training, it's easier to keep going.

Taiki: You **(3)** _____ _____ _____ so easy, Jane. My problem is I just don't like exercising very much.

Jane: Well, I can help you find something you may like. As you know, I've tried lots of different sports and exercises. Do you **(4)** _____ individual sports or team sports?

Taiki: If I had to choose one, I'd go for individual sports. That way I don't have to **(5)** _____ _____ other people. I can do what I want, when I want.

Jane: Right, so that rules out basketball and soccer. How about cycling? That's a great way to exercise, get some fresh air, and you can **(6)** _____ go to new places doing it.

Taiki: What about the rain? Bikes are expensive, too, aren't they? I'm a student like you, so I haven't got a lot of money.

Jane: In that case, you should try swimming. It doesn't matter if it rains then, you'll already be wet! Why don't you do that? You can swim, can't you?

Taiki: Yes. I used to swim a lot **(7)** _____ _____ _____ _____. I'm not as fit as you, though. Do you think it'd be OK to go to the pool even though I'm not in very good shape?

Jane: Of course! Let's go together and I can give you some **(8)** _____ and tips to remind you what to do.

Speaking Practice: Practice the conversation with your partner.

46

IV ‖ Pronunciation Check

イントネーションの違い

英語を話すとき、文末が上がったり下がったりします。

　　Do you like Chinese food? ↗ ［Yes/No を尋ねる疑問文］

　　What is your favorite sport? ↘ ［疑問詞で始まる疑問文］

　　Is it a vegetable (↗) or a fruit? (↘) ［二者択一で尋ねる文］ 最初は上がり、次は下がります。

付加疑問文のイントネーションは、自分が確信を持っているときは下がり、あまり確信がなく相手に返答を求めるときは上がります。

例）It is warm today, isn't it? ↘ （今日は暖かいね）

　　He won the game, didn't he? ↗ （彼は試合に勝ったんだよね）

Exercises

 33

Listen to the recording and mark the correct intonation using ↗ or ↘ in the sentences below. Then, practice saying the sentences, paying attention to intonation.

1. Which do you like better, football or baseball?

2. Why didn't you finish this homework yesterday?

3. He can speak Spanish well, can't he?

V ‖ Focus on Function

Once you've got into the habit, it is easier to keep going.
「一度習慣がつけば、続けるのは簡単だ」

接続詞の once を使って二つの文章をつなげる形で、「一度〜すれば…」という意味を表すことができます。同じ使い方で、「〜するとすぐに…」の意味もあるので、文脈から判断するようにしましょう。

例）Once he gets home, we can go out. （彼が帰ってきたらすぐに出かけます）

Exercises

Complete the sentences below using *once*.

1. そのドラマを一度見始めたら止められないよ。
　　_____ you start watching the TV drama, you _____ _____ .

2. やり方を覚えたら、このゲームは難しくない。
　　This game is not difficult _____ you learn _____ _____
　　_____ .

3. それが修理されたら、前よりもずっと使いやすくなりました。
　　_____ it had been fixed, it was _____ _____ _____ to use.

VI │Find out

In the conversation on p.46, Jane and Taiki talked about sports and exercise. Think about a sport or exercise you have done. Then, write the questions below. Next, write your answers to the questions. Finally, ask a partner the questions and find out what the sport or exercise they have done is.

The sport or exercise you have done: _____	
Q1: (How many times / done) _____?	
You: _____	Your partner: _____
Q2: (Are / member / club) _____?	
You: _____	Your partner: _____
Q3: (When / did / first time) _____?	
You: _____	Your partner: _____
Q4: (Is / individual / team) _____?	
You: _____	Your partner: _____
Q5: Your question: _____?	
You: _____	Your partner: _____
The sport or exercise your partner has done: _____	

Useful Language

Noun phrases: jogging / weight training / yoga / martial arts / stretching / court / pitch / tournament / coach / injury

Verb phrases: I started . . . / I used to . . . / XX helps . . . / I prefer . . .

Adjectives: fun / enjoyable / hard / challenging / relaxing / refreshing / competitive / social

《どのように感じるか話してみよう》

スポーツなど自分がやってみて感じたことを話してみましょう。"It is fun to swim."（泳ぐのは楽しい）のように、形容詞を使って感想を説明することができます。その他にも、"XX is an enjoyable experience." の表現を使って、どのような経験なのかを伝えてみましょう。

UNIT 9

I don't feel so good.
– Talking about Illness

I Vocabulary

Part 1: Match the words (a~j) with their meanings (1~10).

a. symptom	b. thirsty	c. vaccine	d. medicine	e. fever
f. chill	g. catch	h. supplement	i. appetite	j. inject

1. _____ something extra that is added to something
2. _____ to become infected with or affected by (a sickness or disease)
3. _____ a feeling of being cold
4. _____ a desire for food
5. _____ a substance given to a person or animal to protect against a particular disease
6. _____ having an uncomfortable feeling because you need something to drink
7. _____ a substance that is used to treat a disease or relieve pain
8. _____ a change in the body or mind which indicates that a disease is present
9. _____ a body temperature that is higher than normal
10. _____ to force a liquid medicine into someone's body by using a special needle

Part 2: Complete the dialogs with words from Part 1.

1. **A:** Do you have a good diet?
   B: Not really. I eat too much fast food. But I take a vitamin _____ every day.
2. **A:** Are you okay? You don't look good.
   B: I think I have a cold.
   A: Well, don't come too close. I don't want to _____ it!
3. **A:** I have a headache. Maybe I have influenza.
   B: I don't think so. Your headache is a(n) _____ of using your phone too much.
4. **A:** Okay, Mr. Bowden, I'm going to _____ the vaccine into your arm.
   B: Oh no. I really don't like needles. Will it hurt?
   A: You'll be fine. You'll just feel a little prick, and it will all be over.
5. **A:** Do you eat well?
   B: Yes, I do. I do a lot of exercise, so I always have a good _____.

🔊 **Listening Practice:** Listen to two people talking about illnesses they have experienced. Write the illnesses and check (✔) the correct boxes.

1. Illness: _____

	Yes	No
had a fever	☐	☐
had no appetite	☐	☐
needed medicine	☐	☐
will get a vaccine	☐	☐

2. Illness: _____

	Yes	No
had a fever	☐	☐
had no appetite	☐	☐
needed medicine	☐	☐
will get a vaccine	☐	☐

🔊 **Speaking Practice:** What do you think is important for preventing illness? Check the boxes below and talk to your partner about how they stay healthy.

	Very important	Quite important	Not important	Reason
avoiding stress	☐	☐	☐	_____
eating well	☐	☐	☐	_____
doing exercise	☐	☐	☐	_____
taking supplements	☐	☐	☐	_____
getting vaccinated	☐	☐	☐	_____

Useful Language

Questions
- Do you . . . ?
- What do you do to . . . ?
- Do you have . . . ?
- What are your symptoms?
- When did it start?

Answers
- I have . . .
- I feel . . .
- It started when I . . .

Details
- Symptoms (have): a cough / a runny nose / diarrhea / a rash / a fever
- Symptoms (feel): nauseous / dizzy / faint / weak / tired / chilly

Notes

You have to have a balanced diet.

日本語で「ダイエット」と言うと減量を思い浮かべる人が多いと思います。diet は「日常の食事」を意味する語で、"a healthy diet" は「健康的な食事」という表現です。痩せることを目的とした「ダイエットをする」は、"be on a diet" を使います。

III Conversation

Part 1: Listen to the conversation and choose the most appropriate answer (a~d) for each question.

Get the gist

1. What is implied in the conversation?
   - **a.** Momoko is sick.
   - **b.** Lee is sick.
   - **c.** Both Momoko and Lee are sick.
   - **d.** Neither Momoko nor Lee are sick.

2. How does Momoko probably feel during the conversation?
   - **a.** Scared
   - **b.** Hungry
   - **c.** Concerned
   - **d.** Cold

Get the details

1. Which of the following symptoms does Lee not have?
   - **a.** Tiredness
   - **b.** Fever
   - **c.** Weakness
   - **d.** Headache

2. How does Lee feel about using Momoko's blanket?
   - **a.** He doesn't want to.
   - **b.** He feels sleepy.
   - **c.** He feels excited.
   - **d.** He is happy to.

3. What has Lee been doing?
   - **a.** Drinking enough
   - **b.** Eating enough
   - **c.** Sleeping enough
   - **d.** Seeing a doctor

4. Why does Momoko think Lee should see a doctor?
   - **a.** Because he hasn't been eating enough.
   - **b.** Because he has been sleeping too much.
   - **c.** Because he may be sick.
   - **d.** Because he may have a cold.

5. What will Lee probably do next?
   - **a.** Go to the doctor
   - **b.** Go to sleep
   - **c.** Eat some food
   - **d.** Sit down and rest

Part 2: Listen to the conversation again and write the missing words or phrases in the spaces.

Momoko: And we're done for the day! Time to relax.

Lee: Mmm.

Momoko: What's wrong, Lee? You (1) _____ _____ _____.

Lee: I don't feel so good. I feel really tired and weak, and I have a bad (2) _____.

Momoko: Oh no. I'm sorry to hear that. You need to take care of yourself. Here, sit down and rest. Now, what other (3) _____ do you have? Do you have a fever?

Lee: Thanks, Momoko. I'm (4) _____ _____ _____ I have a fever. I don't think so, but I feel cold.

Momoko: Oh dear. That doesn't sound good. Why don't you use my blanket? I don't need it right now.

Lee: Thanks again, Momoko. I really appreciate it.

Momoko: No worries. How is your (5) _____? Have you been eating okay?

Lee: I haven't eaten anything since lunch yesterday, so I'm (6) _____ _____ _____ right now.

Momoko: Oh. So, you are feeling tired, weak, and chilly. And you haven't eaten for nearly a day and a half? Are you feeling thirsty? And have you been sleeping well?

Lee: No, I've been drinking plenty of water. But I only got about two hours of sleep last night.

Momoko: Only two hours? That's really worrying. (7) _____ _____ _____ you may have caught the flu. I think you should see a doctor and make sure. It's better to be safe than sorry.

Lee: Thank you for your concern, but I don't think I have the flu. I was playing a really exciting game last night, and I forgot to sleep. And I'm on a diet, so I'm only eating one (8) _____ a day. I think maybe that's why I feel so bad. I'll be fine once I've had lunch and a nap. But thank you for letting me use your blanket.

Speaking Practice: Practice the conversation with your partner.

IV Pronunciation Check

リダクション：消える音 p

Unit 3 では消える音 t について学びました。p もリダクションが生じる場合があります。"symptom" のように、単語の中にある p の音は聞こえにくくなります。他にも、"step" などの語で p が文末や語句の最後にくるとき、または次の単語が子音で始まるときは、聞こえにくくなることがあります。例）He lives on the top floor.［p の音はほとんど発音されていないように聞こえます］

Exercises

 37

Listen to the recording and choose the sentence which uses reduction, A or B. Then, practice saying the sentences, paying attention to reduction.

1. I cannot stop eating this popcorn.   A   B

2. Ryan flipped open his laptop computer.   A   B

3. She made many attempts to get medical help.   A   B

V Focus on Function

I'm not sure if I have a fever.「熱があるかわかりません」

はっきりとしたことが言えない場合、"I'm not sure if . . ."「〜かどうかわかりません」という表現が使えます。この if は「もし〜ならば」ではなく、「〜であるかどうか」という意味になります。if の後ろには主語＋動詞が続きます。自分個人ではなくグループの考えとして話すときには、I を We に変えることもできます。

Exercises

Complete the sentences below using *not sure*.

1. 彼が明日来るかどうかわかりません。
   I'm _____ _____ _____ he will _____ _____.

2. 新しい案が前のものより良いのかわかりません。
   We _____ _____ _____ _____ the new plan is
   _____ _____ the previous one.

3. カレンがまだその会社に勤めているのかわかりません。
   I'm _____ _____ _____ Karen still _____ for the
   company.

VI │ Find out

In the conversation on p.52, Momoko and Lee talked about illness. Think about an illness that you had. Then, write the questions below. Next, write your answers to the questions. Finally, ask a partner the questions and find out what the illness they had was.

The illness you chose: _____	
Q1: (How many times / have / had) _____ ?	
You: _____	Your partner: _____
Q2: (Did / have / fever) _____ ?	
You: _____	Your partner: _____
Q3: (How / was / appetite) _____ ?	
You: _____	Your partner: _____
Q4: (Did / have / headache) _____ ?	
You: _____	Your partner: _____
Q5: Your question: _____ ?	
You: _____	Your partner: _____
The illness your partner chose: _____	

Useful Language

Noun phrases: hospital / doctor / pharmacist / medicine / prescription / injection
Verb phrases: suffer from . . . / have a . . . pain / heal / prescribe / be allergic to . . . / inject / catch
Adjectives: sharp / terrible / awful / constant / dull / stabbing / pricking / occasional

《症状を話してみよう》
痛みについて説明するには、"I have a . . . pain" を使います。どのような痛みなのかは形容詞で表現しましょう。例えば、「お腹がひどく痛みます」と言う場合は、"I have a terrible pain in my stomach." となります。アレルギーがある場合は、"I'm allergic to . . ." を使います。

UNIT 10

Why do you do that?
– Talking about Culture

I Vocabulary

Part 1: Match the words (a~j) with their meanings (1~10).

| a. tradition | b. visit | c. religion | d. serve | e. move |
| f. invite | g. occasion | h. custom | i. throw | j. flat |

1. _____ a system of beliefs, ceremonies, and rules used to worship a god or a group of gods
2. _____ to ask someone to go somewhere or do something
3. _____ an action or way of behaving that is usual among people in a particular group or place
4. _____ an apartment typically on one floor
5. _____ to give food or drink to someone at a meal
6. _____ a special event or time
7. _____ a way of thinking or behaving that has been used by people for a long time
8. _____ to go somewhere to see a person or place
9. _____ to go to a different place to live
10. _____ to organize and hold (a party)

Part 2: Complete the dialogs with words from Part 1.

1. **A:** We're throwing a party for Judy tonight. Here's your invitation. Can you come?
   B: I'd love to. What's the _____?
   A: It's her birthday.
2. **A:** Teacher! How are American English and British English different?
   B: That's a good question. Well, some words are different. For example, Americans say "apartment," but British people say "_____".
3. **A:** My weekend? I'm a Christian, so I go to church on Sunday mornings. How about you, Mohammed?
   B: Oh, my _____ is Islam, so I visit a mosque every Friday evening.
4. **A:** How about this restaurant?
   B: I don't know. Do they _____ vegetarian food?
5. **A:** In Japan, we use *jan ken* to make decisions. How about in England?
   B: Oh, the _____ in England is to toss a coin. We usually toss a coin to see who will start with the ball in a soccer or rugby game.

II ‖ Warm-up for Listening & Speaking

 38, 39

🔹 **Listening Practice:** Listen to two people talking about customs in their countries. Write the countries and check (✔) the correct boxes.

1. Country: _____

	Yes	No
has two kinds of time	☐	☐
can be 30 minutes late	☐	☐
leaving early is okay	☐	☐
Japan is different	☐	☐

2. Country: _____

	Yes	No
has two kinds of people	☐	☐
has religious food rules	☐	☐
can serve chicken	☐	☐
nasi lemak is great	☐	☐

🔹 **Speaking Practice:** Which of the Japanese customs below do you think are important? Check the boxes below and talk to your partner about customs.

	Very important	Quite important	Not important	Reason
Hatsumode	☐	☐	☐	_____
Otoshidama	☐	☐	☐	_____
Fukubukuro	☐	☐	☐	_____
Setsubun	☐	☐	☐	_____
Hanami	☐	☐	☐	_____

Useful Language

Questions
- What do you think is important in your . . . ?
- How are A and B different?
- Have you ever experienced a different culture?
- What's your favorite [festival]?

Answers
- XX is important because . . .
- For example, we . . .
- Yes, I have. / No, I haven't.
- My favorite [festival] is . . . because . . .

Details
- Culture: greeting / food / ceremony / attire / house / communication / school / art / religion

Notes
For example, . . .
文化の違いなどを説明するとき、具体例を示すと伝わりやすくなります。"For example" はよく使う表現ですが、"Take XX for example."（〜を例に挙げてみましょう）や、"To give an example."（一例を挙げます）なども覚えておくと便利です。

III ‖Conversation

 40

Part 1: Listen to the conversation and choose the most appropriate answer (a~d) for each question.

▎ Get the gist

1. What can we infer about Momo?
    - **a.** She has just moved.
    - **b.** She lives with Nick.
    - **c.** She is friends with Nick and Natasha.
    - **d.** She will travel to Russia with Natasha.

2. What are they mainly talking about?
    - **a.** Customs and traditions about gifts
    - **b.** Customs and traditions about food
    - **c.** Customs and traditions about moving home
    - **d.** Customs and traditions about pets

▎ Get the details

1. Why was Nick surprised?
    - **a.** Because Momo is his new neighbor.
    - **b.** Because Natasha has a pet cat.
    - **c.** Because he moved into a new flat.
    - **d.** Because he got a present.

2. What did Momo tell Nick about giving presents?
    - **a.** That Japan is opposite to New Zealand. **b.** That it was a Japanese custom.
    - **c.** That it was a tradition in New Zealand. **d.** That Natasha told her to do it.

3. What does Nick say people do when they throw a housewarming party?
    - **a.** They visit their new neighbors.
    - **b.** They let a cat enter a new home first.
    - **c.** They buy a new broom.
    - **d.** They invite their new neighbors to visit.

4. What did Natasha inform Momo about?
    - **a.** An old English tradition
    - **b.** A Russian custom
    - **c.** A New Zealand tradition
    - **d.** A Japanese custom

5. What might Momo do the next time she moves?
    - **a.** Buy a new broom
    - **b.** Give her neighbor a hand towel
    - **c.** Get a pet cat
    - **d.** Throw a housewarming party

Part 2: Listen to the conversation again and write the missing words or phrases in the spaces.

Nick: Hi, Momo. Can I (1) _____ _____ _____ _____?

Momo: Sure, Nick, how can I help you? Is everything okay?

Nick: Oh, yes, everything is fine. But yesterday, my new neighbor knocked on my door and gave me a small present. But I don't know why they did that. Can you tell me?

Momo: Was it a hand (2) _____?

Nick: Yes, it was! (3) _____ _____ _____ _____?

Momo: It's a Japanese tradition. It's a way of getting to know your neighbors when you move to a new place. Not so many people do it (4) _____, though.

Nick: Ah, I see. We (5) _____ _____ _____ tradition in New Zealand, but it's in reverse.

Momo: I don't understand. What do you mean when you say it's in reverse?

Nick: Well, when you move into a new house or flat, you (6) _____ a party and invite your friends and new neighbors. All the guests bring some food or something useful or fun for your new home. We call it a housewarming party.

Momo: Oh, I see. Yes, that is the opposite to Japan, isn't it? Do you (7) _____ _____ _____ when you move somewhere new in New Zealand?

Nick: Well, an old English custom is to buy a new broom when you move. I think the idea is to start your new life fresh and clean.

Momo: I like that idea. Maybe I'll do it when I move next. Actually, Natasha told me that in Russia it's traditional to let a cat enter your new home first. It's supposed to bring you good luck. She even told me that if you don't have a cat, you can (8) _____ one.

Speaking Practice: Practice the conversation with your partner.

IV ⎟Pronunciation Check

カタカナでの発音

英語の単語がカタカナ表記になって、日本語独自の発音になっている言葉があります。「タオル」は英語で towel【táuəl】と発音するので、カタカナ表記の発音でタオルと言っても通じません。アクセントをつける場所が日本語と英語で違う場合もあります。このような単語は日常生活のなかでたくさんあるので、日頃から意識して英語の発音をチェックしてみるようにしましょう。

Exercises

EC CD 41

Listen to the recording and write the words you hear. Then, practice saying the sentences, paying attention to pronunciation.

1. We'll go to the _____ _____ , wearing matching _____ .

2. May I order? I'll have an _____-free _____ .

3. Michel received the first dose of the _____ for the harmful _____ .

V ⎟Focus on Function

It's supposed to bring you good luck. 「幸運をもたらしてくれるよ」

"be supposed to" は「〜することになっている、〜だと思われている」という意味で使われます。約束や規則、義務に関する表現で、軽い命令を示すこともあります。日常会話でよく出てきますが、日本語に訳すときは文脈によってかなり変わってくるので、ニュアンスを確認しておきましょう。

Exercises

Complete the sentences below using *be supposed to*.

1. ドロシーは9時に来るはずだよ。
    Dorothy _____ _____ _____ arrive at 9 o'clock.

2. 彼が昨晩電話してくれることになっていたんだけど。
    He _____ _____ _____ call me last night.

3. この部屋で煙草を吸ってはいけません。
    You _____ _____ _____ _____ smoke in this room.

VI │ Find out

In the conversation on p.58, Nick and Momo talked about customs. Think about a custom that you like. Then, write the questions below. Next, write your answers to the questions. Finally, ask a partner the questions and find out what the custom they like is.

The custom you like: _____	
Q1: (When) _____?	
You: _____	Your partner: _____
Q2: (Where) _____?	
You: _____	Your partner: _____
Q3: (What / do) _____?	
You: _____	Your partner: _____
Q4: (Why / do) _____?	
You: _____	Your partner: _____
Q5: Your question: _____?	
You: _____	Your partner: _____
The custom your partner likes: _____	

Useful Language

Noun phrases: seasonal event / present / celebration / hospitality / festival / occasion
Verb phrases: develop / spread / bring / adapt / follow / observe
Adjectives: traditional / common / ancestral / ethnic / peculiar / significant / important

《文化や慣習について話してみよう》

「日本では〜します」と言うには、"In Japan, we . . ." の形で動詞は現在形を使って表現することができますが、昔の慣習などを話す場合は、"Japanese people used to . . ."（〈日本人は〉かつて〜する習わしだった）となります。その他にも、"According to (a) . . . custom"（〜の慣習に従って）という表現も使ってみましょう。

UNIT 11

It's a special day.
– Talking about Holidays and Festivals

I | Vocabulary

Part 1: Match the words (a~j) with their meanings (1~10).

a. celebrate	b. festival	c. fireworks	d. crowded	e. gift
f. regional	g. national	h. decorations	i. relationships	j. neighbors

1. _____ belonging to an area of a country
2. _____ belonging to a whole country
3. _____ objects put up on special occasions
4. _____ connections that people have with each other
5. _____ very busy, many people
6. _____ people who live near each other
7. _____ something given to another person
8. _____ colorful controlled explosions used in displays or in celebrations
9. _____ to recognize or acknowledge something special with a party or enjoyable activity
10. _____ a special event or celebration

Part 2: Complete the dialogs with words from Part 1.

1. **A:** Are you going to the festival this weekend?
   B: No. Too many people will be there. It's always so _____.
2. **A:** What are you shopping for?
   B: A Valentine's _____ for my boyfriend. It's difficult to know what to get him, though.
3. **A:** Why do you like your local festival?
   B: It helps to build better _____ with our neighbors. We can get to know each other a lot better.
4. **A:** Do you think your country should have more _____ holidays?
   B: No, Japan has enough already. I don't think we need any more.
5. **A:** What do you like most about summer festivals?
   B: Definitely the _____. They're so beautiful in the night sky.

II Warm-up for Listening & Speaking 42, 43

■ **Listening Practice:** Listen to two people talking about different holidays or special events. Write the events and check (✔) the correct boxes.

1. Event: _____

	Yes	No
is a Japanese event	☐	☐
celebrates it with friends	☐	☐
eats special food	☐	☐
has plans for next year	☐	☐

2. Event: _____

	Yes	No
is a Japanese event	☐	☐
celebrates it with friends	☐	☐
eats special food	☐	☐
has plans for next year	☐	☐

■ **Speaking Practice:** What do you think is important when celebrating national holidays? Check the boxes below and talk to your partner about celebrating national holidays.

	Very important	Quite important	Not important	Reason
eating special food	☐	☐	☐	_____
talking with family	☐	☐	☐	_____
meeting neighbors	☐	☐	☐	_____
watching TV	☐	☐	☐	_____
going to shrines	☐	☐	☐	_____

Useful Language

Questions
- What do you usually do on . . . ?
- Is there a festival in . . . ?
- Do you know the meaning of . . . ?

Answers
- We usually . . .
- A festival is held in/at . . .
- XX stands for . . .

Details
- Holidays: Easter / Thanksgiving / Coming-of-Age Day / Independence Day / the Emperor's Birthday / Constitution Day / Boxing Day

Notes

We celebrate Christmas with a party.

祝日などを何か（イベント／方法／もの など）で祝うときは celebrate ＋祝日＋ with ～の形で表します。「独立記念日を 花火でお祝いする」は "We celebrate Independence Day with fireworks." となります。with の後ろには名詞が続く ので注意しましょう。

III ‖Conversation

 44

Part 1: Listen to the conversation and choose the most appropriate answer (a~d) for each question.

Get the gist

1. Where are Honoka and Alex most likely?
   - **a.** At university
   - **b.** At home
   - **c.** In Nagasaki
   - **d.** In New Zealand

2. Who is Alex most likely?
   - **a.** A teacher
   - **b.** A full-time worker
   - **c.** An international student
   - **d.** A university staff member

Get the details

1. What will Alex do in the winter vacation?
   - **a.** He hasn't decided yet.
   - **b.** Go to Nagasaki.
   - **c.** Go to New Zealand.
   - **d.** Go to a local shrine.

2. Who will Honoka spend time with over the winter vacation?
   - **a.** Just her friends
   - **b.** Just her family
   - **c.** Both her friends and family
   - **d.** Alex

3. What will Honoka do at the shrine on January 1st?
   - **a.** Have classes
   - **b.** Pray for a successful new year
   - **c.** Party with friends
   - **d.** Show Alex around

4. What does Alex say about New Year's Eve in New Zealand?
   - **a.** It's better.
   - **b.** It's not as good.
   - **c.** It's very different from in Japan.
   - **d.** It's the same as in Japan.

5. For how many days does Nagasaki Lantern Festival last?
   - **a.** 10
   - **b.** 15
   - **c.** 15,000
   - **d.** 8

Part 2: Listen to the conversation again and write the missing words or phrases in the spaces.

Honoka: The winter vacation is coming soon, Alex. What are you (1) _____ to do?

Alex: To be honest Honoka, I haven't decided, yet. I've (2) _____ _____ _____ study and work so I haven't had much time to think about it. How about you?

Honoka: I'm going to go back to Nagasaki. We won't have classes here at the university for a (3) _____, so I'll be able to go back for around ten days.

Alex: That sounds nice. I wish I could see my family over new year, but going all the way back to New Zealand is a bit harder than going to Nagasaki! What (4) _____ _____ _____ _____ for New Year?

Honoka: I stay at home with my family on New Year's Eve and watch TV. Then, on the morning of January 1st we all go to the local shrine and pray for a (5) _____ new year.

Alex: Oh. Are you religious? I didn't know that.

Honoka: No. I'm not religious. It's just a tradition. (6) _____ _____ _____ _____ like that?

Alex: No. I usually spend New Year's Eve in New Zealand partying with friends. It's a totally different experience to tell the truth. Do you spend any time with friends over the New Year holiday?

Honoka: Well, it's related to Chinese New Year, not Japanese New Year, but there's a 15-day festival called Nagasaki Lantern Festival. I go there with my friends. Over 15,000 lanterns get lit all around the city. Some of the (7) _____ can be as big as eight meters!

Alex: Wow! That sounds great. I've never been to Nagasaki before, but I'd like to go one day.

Honoka: You've never been to Nagasaki? Maybe (8) _____ _____ _____ _____ one day and I could show you around.

Speaking Practice: Practice the conversation with your partner.

IV Pronunciation Check

つながる音を聞き取ろう Part 2

Unit 7 では、子音＋母音のつながる音について学びました。つながる音には子音＋子音や母音＋母音のパターンもあります。次の箇所は音がつながって発音されているように聞こえます。

例）Did you see Ken yesterday？ ［子音＋子音］
　　Please, go ahead. ［母音＋母音］
つながる音に注意することで、リスニングもスピーキングも上達していきます。

Exercises

 45

📢 **Listen to the recording and mark the linking part using (‿). Then, practice saying the sentences, paying attention to linking.**

1. Thank you very much. We had a good time.

2. Kevin fell on hard times this year.

3. I need to buy flour and butter because I'm going to bake an apple pie.

V Focus on Function

On the morning of January 1st「1 月 1 日の朝に」

日付、時間、曜日など時を示す前置詞の使い方を覚えておきましょう。特定の日付や曜日は on を用います。午前・午後は in the morning / in the afternoon となりますが、「何月何日の朝」などは on になります。月や季節、年は in、時刻やある特定の期間は at を使います。

例）on Monday / in summer / at nine p.m.

Exercises

📢 **Complete the sentences below using prepositions.**

1. **A:** Could you pick me up _____ the morning?
   B: Sure. I'll come and get you _____ 10 o'clock.

2. Today's meeting finished _____ noon. The next one has been arranged
   _____ the afternoon of November 17.

3. _____ May 26, Ike left Tokyo for London. He'll go back to Japan
   _____ July.

VI │ Find out

In the conversation on p.64, Honoka and Alex talked about holidays and special events. Think about a holiday or special event that you like. Then, write the questions below. Next, write your answers to the questions. Finally, ask a partner the questions and find out what the holiday or special event they like is.

The holiday or special event you like: _____
Q1: (Is / traditional Japanese) _____ ?
You: _____ | Your partner: _____
Q2: (How / celebrate) _____ ?
You: _____ | Your partner: _____
Q3: (Who / celebrate / with) _____ ?
You: _____ | Your partner: _____
Q4: (When / celebrate) _____ ?
You: _____ | Your partner: _____
Q5: Your question: _____ ?
You: _____ | Your partner: _____
The holiday or special event your partner likes: _____

Useful Language

Noun phrases: festival / parade / gift / costume / ceremony / decoration / food / relationship

Verb phrases: sing / dance / (be) held / see / eat / decorate / display / drink / play / put on

Adjectives: special / traditional / religious / seasonal / annual / ritual / solemn / crowded / regional / national

《行事について説明してみよう》
祝日や祭りは、その国の文化や歴史と深く関わっています。どのように祝うのか、何を意味しているのか、英語で尋ねたり説明したりしてみましょう。「〜は何のためなのですか？」は "What is/are XX for?" という表現が使えます。"It is said that . . ." （〜と言われています）を使って意味などを説明することができます。

UNIT 12

Are you going anywhere?
– Talking about Travel and Vacations

I ‖ Vocabulary

🔲 **Part 1: Match the words and phrases (a~j) with their meanings (1~10).**

a. beach	b. boss	c. wedding	d. arrive	e. event
f. miss	g. get married	h. culture	i. traditional	j. fly

1. _____ based on a way of thinking or behaving that has been used by people for a long time
2. _____ a ceremony at which two people are married to each other
3. _____ to become the husband or wife of someone
4. _____ an area covered with sand or small rocks that is next to an ocean, a sea, or a lake
5. _____ a planned occasion or activity
6. _____ to move through the air very quickly
7. _____ to come to or reach a place after traveling
8. _____ the beliefs, customs, arts, etc., of a particular society, group, place, or time
9. _____ a manager, a supervisor
10. _____ to arrive too late for (something or someone)

🔲 **Part 2: Complete the dialogs with words and phrases from Part 1.**

1. **A:** What's your dream wedding, Yuki?
   B: Oh, I want to have a _____ Japanese wedding when I get married. I'd love to wear a wedding kimono.
2. **A:** What are your vacation plans, James?
   B: I'm going to Thailand this year. I'm going to swim in the sea, lie on the _____, and just relax.
3. **A:** I want to know more about British _____ and history. But I don't know where to go.
   B: You should definitely visit the British Museum. You can learn a lot about Britain there.
4. **A:** Are you going anywhere this weekend?
   B: No, I can't. My _____ said I have to work.
5. **A:** I'll _____ in Japan on April 2nd. Is that a good time?
   B: Yes, that's great. We can go to *hanami*. It's one of the biggest events in Japan.

II Warm-up for Listening & Speaking

 46, 47

🔊 **Listening Practice:** Listen to two people talking about their vacations. Write the vacation activities and check (✔) the correct boxes.

1. Activity: _____

	Yes	No
went to 3 countries	☐	☐
saw family members	☐	☐
got married	☐	☐
missed a plane	☐	☐

2. Activity: _____

	Yes	No
went to 3 countries	☐	☐
saw family members	☐	☐
got married	☐	☐
missed a plane	☐	☐

🔊 **Speaking Practice:** Which of the following are important to you when traveling? Check the boxes below and talk to your partner about travel and vacations.

	Very important	Quite important	Not important	Reason
beautiful views	☐	☐	☐	_____
traditional culture	☐	☐	☐	_____
exciting events	☐	☐	☐	_____
good food	☐	☐	☐	_____
interesting places	☐	☐	☐	_____

Useful Language

Questions
- Have you ever been to . . . ?
- What countries would you like to visit?
- How are you planning to spend your vacations?

Answers
- Yes, I have. / No, I haven't.
- I've been to . . .
- I'd like to visit . . .
- I'm planning to . . .

Details
- Activities: surfing / climbing / visiting museums / camping / reading books / cooking

Notes

on my vacation

休暇中のことを話すときは "on my vacation" や "during the vacation" などの表現を使ってみましょう。具体的に伝える場合には、"the Christmas vacation" や "a ski vacation"（スキーを楽しむ休暇）といった言い方をします。

III Conversation

 48

Part 1: Listen to the conversation and choose the most appropriate answer (a~d) for each question.

Get the gist

1. What can we infer about Daniel?
   - **a.** He is friends with Roxana and Simone.
   - **b.** He is friends with Roxana but not with Simone.
   - **c.** He is friends with Simone but not with Roxana.
   - **d.** He is not friends with either Simone or Roxana.

2. How does Daniel probably feel about the Bali trip?
   - **a.** Excited
   - **b.** Happy
   - **c.** Jealous
   - **d.** Angry

Get the details

1. When does this conversation most likely take place?
   - **a.** August 1st
   - **b.** August 3rd
   - **c.** August 22nd
   - **d.** September 1st

2. Where will Roxana go in the summer vacation?
   - **a.** Miyakojima
   - **b.** Bali
   - **c.** Narita
   - **d.** Okinawa

3. Which of the following statements about Roxana is correct?
   - **a.** She will travel with Simone.
   - **b.** She will stay with Daniel's family.
   - **c.** She will stay with Simone's family.
   - **d.** She will travel with Daniel.

4. Who is Simone most likely?
   - **a.** Daniel and Roxana's classmate
   - **b.** Daniel and Roxana's teacher
   - **c.** Daniel and Roxana's student
   - **d.** Daniel and Roxana's boss

5. Which of the following statements about Daniel is not correct?
   - **a.** He is a student.
   - **b.** He will travel to Bali.
   - **c.** He is from Okinawa.
   - **d.** He works with his parents.

Part 2: Listen to the conversation again and write the missing words or phrases in the spaces.

Roxana: And that's our last lesson of the semester! See you on (1) _____ 1st, Daniel.

Daniel: (2) _____ _____ _____, Roxana. Where are you going?

Roxana: Didn't I tell you? I'm flying to Bali for three weeks of sun, sea, and (3) _____ food. I leave tonight from Narita and I'll be back on August 22nd.

Daniel: No, you didn't tell me! Are you (4) _____ _____ _____?

Roxana: Well, I'm (5) _____ to Bali by myself. But I'm going to stay with Simone and her mother when I get there.

Daniel: Simone? Oh, she's from Indonesia, isn't she? Now I understand. I hope you have a great time. I wish I was going with you.

Roxana: Thanks, Daniel. How about you? Are (6) _____ _____ _____ in the summer vacation?

Daniel: Yes, I am. I'll be in Okinawa for all six weeks of the summer vacation. I'm leaving (7) _____ _____ _____ _____, on the 3rd.

Roxana: Oh, wow. That sounds great. So, you'll be having a beach holiday, too!

Daniel: I'll be on the beach, but it won't be a holiday. I'm from Okinawa, and my parents run a surfing (8) _____ on a beach on Miyakojima. So, I'll be working there through the summer vacation. All of it. I have to work there every vacation. Working with my mom's great, but my dad is a tough boss.

Roxana: That must be hard. But . . . it's Okinawa! Hey, Simone! Let's visit Daniel in Okinawa when we get back from Bali!

Daniel: Yes, please visit me. You can stay with my family . . . and help us in the shop.

Speaking Practice: Practice the conversation with your partner.

IV Pronunciation Check

アクセントの位置

英語のアクセントの位置には、ある程度のパターンがあります。接尾語が以下のような語は、その直前にある母音にアクセントを置きます。アクセントが違うと通じないこともあるので、正しい位置に付けるよう気をつけましょう。

○接尾語が -ic / -ion / ian / -ity / -ious の語

例）fantastic ［-ic の直前の母音 a にアクセントを置く］

＊例外　television は -ion の直前ではなく、最初の e にアクセントを置きます。

Exercises

 49

Listen to the recording and mark the correct stress using (✔) in the underlined words below. Then, practice saying the sentences, paying attention to stress.

1. He was an <u>academic</u> at a music college before becoming a famous <u>musician</u>.

2. Natalia has an intense <u>curiosity</u> about the unexplored <u>regions</u> of Mars.

3. We had dinner at a <u>luxurious</u> restaurant to celebrate the <u>occasion</u>.

V Focus on Function

That must be hard. 「きっと大変だろね」

助動詞の must は、「～しなければならない」と話者の主観で義務や必要を強く示す意味があります（have to は客観的な必要性を表すときに使います）。must には他にも「きっと～のはずだ」と推量を示す意味もあります。must の否定形 mustn't は、禁止の意味になります。

例）You must arrive on time. （時間どおりに着かなくてはいけないよ）

　　You must be joking.　　（冗談を言っているのですよね）

また、can は「できる」の他に、可能性を表す「～のことがある」や、否定形で「～のはずがない」という推量を示すので、こちらもチェックしておきましょう。

Exercises

Look at the sentences below and circle the correct words.

1. Jessie looks awful. She (**must / can**) be tired.

2. Really? I don't believe you. It (**mustn't / can't**) be true.

3. He (**must / can**) have arrived by now.

VI Find out

In the conversation on p.70, Roxana and Daniel talked about their summer vacation trips. Think about a place you would like to visit. Then, write the questions below. Next, write your answers to the questions. Finally, ask a partner the questions and find out what the place they would like to visit is.

The place you would like to visit: _____	
Q1: (in / Japan) _____?	
You: _____	Your partner: _____
Q2: (Have / been / before) _____?	
You: _____	Your partner: _____
Q3: (Why / want / go) _____?	
You: _____	Your partner: _____
Q4: (What / do / there) _____?	
You: _____	Your partner: _____
Q5: Your question: _____?	
You: _____	Your partner: _____
The place your partner would like to visit: _____	

Useful Language

Noun phrases: train / airplane / hotel / cottage / seaside / countryside / tour / souvenir

Verb phrases: take / stay / see / leave / visit / join / arrive / enjoy / spend / eat

Adjectives: pleasant / exciting / restful / relaxed / economical / luxurious / interesting

《旅行について話してみよう》

"travel" という単語を聞くと、日本語の「旅行」という名詞が思い浮かぶと思いますが、この単語は名詞と動詞の働きをします。動詞としては、"She traveled around the world."（彼女は世界中を旅行した）のように使います。日常会話では動詞を使うことのほうが多く、名詞としては space travel（宇宙旅行）や during one's travels（旅行中に）のような使い方をします。

UNIT 13

I've never done that before.
– Talking about Experiences

I | Vocabulary

Part 1: Match the words (a~j) with their meanings (1~10).

| a. equipment | b. seen | c. someday | d. frightened | e. experience |
| f. alone | g. regret | h. prize | i. venue | j. participate |

1. _____ a feeling of sadness or disappointment about something you have or have not done
2. _____ something given as a reward
3. _____ an unknown time in the future
4. _____ to take part in an action, activity, or event
5. _____ by oneself
6. _____ witnessed, viewed
7. _____ items needed to do something
8. _____ an event or occurrence that leaves an impression on someone
9. _____ scared
10. _____ a place where something happens

Part 2: Complete the dialogs with words from Part 1.

1. **A:** Have you ever been to Africa?
   B: No, but I'd love to go _____. I'm not sure when, but it's definitely on the list of things I most want to do.
2. **A:** Why don't you try a bungee jump?
   B: No way! I'd be too _____. I don't like the feeling of going down in an elevator, so a bungee jump is out of the question.
3. **A:** Would you ever go traveling _____?
   B: I already have. I went around Europe by myself last year. It was an amazing experience. I really recommend it.
4. **A:** Have you ever _____ a lion?
   B: Only in a zoo. Wouldn't it be amazing to see one in the wild, though?
5. **A:** I think we should try to do as many new things as we can.
   B: I agree. I think we only really _____ the things we don't try. I certainly wish I'd done more when I was at university.

📌 **Listening Practice:** People are talking about things they have done recently. Write the activities and check (✔) the correct boxes.

1. Activity: _____

	Yes	No
needed training	☐	☐
was expensive	☐	☐
did it alone	☐	☐
would do it again	☐	☐

2. Activity: _____

	Yes	No
needed training	☐	☐
was expensive	☐	☐
did it alone	☐	☐
would do it again	☐	☐

📌 **Speaking Practice:** Which of the activities below would you like to try? Check the boxes below and talk to your partner about what they would like to try.

	Want to try	So-so	Don't want to try	Reason
ride a horse	☐	☐	☐	_____
touch a snake	☐	☐	☐	_____
go scuba diving	☐	☐	☐	_____
do a bungee jump	☐	☐	☐	_____
climb Mt. Fuji	☐	☐	☐	_____

Useful Language

Questions
- Have you ever been . . . ?
- What is your . . . experience?
- What type of activity do you like to do?

Answers
- Yes, I have. / No, I haven't.
- My . . . experience was when . . .
- I like to . . .

Details
- Experiences: doing a part-time job / attending a ceremony / helping someone / being surprised by something / entering a contest / winning a prize / playing an exciting sport

Notes
From my experience
経験を話すとき、"from my experience"（私の経験から）や "through experience"（経験を通して）などの表現が使えます。「～としての経験がありますか?」と尋ねるには、"Do you have any experience as . . . ?"と as の後に職業などを続けます。

III ‖ Conversation

🎧 52

Part 1: Listen to the conversation and choose the most appropriate answer (a~d) for each question.

Get the gist

1. What can we infer about Taku?
    - **a.** He likes to do many things.
    - **b.** He likes to stay at home.
    - **c.** He likes to spend money on guitars.
    - **d.** He likes to train at gyms.

2. How can we describe Natasha and Taku's relationship?
    - **a.** Distant
    - **b.** Very close
    - **c.** Friendly
    - **d.** Unfriendly

Get the details

1. What is true of Natasha and Taku?
    - **a.** They haven't seen each other recently.
    - **b.** They have seen each other recently.
    - **c.** They have been doing similar things.
    - **d.** They have both joined a new college.

2. How does Taku describe the driving course he did?
    - **a.** Interesting
    - **b.** Difficult
    - **c.** Easy
    - **d.** Relaxing

3. What will Natasha probably do in her new band?
    - **a.** Play the guitar
    - **b.** Play the keyboard
    - **c.** Sing
    - **d.** Play the drums

4. Where did Natasha meet the other members of the new band she will start?
    - **a.** At a driving school
    - **b.** At a college
    - **c.** At a gym
    - **d.** At a music venue

5. Which of the following has Natasha done recently?
    - **a.** Started to play in a band
    - **b.** Joined a new college
    - **c.** Started a kickboxing class
    - **d.** Become a manager

52

Part 2: Listen to the conversation again and write the missing words or phrases in the spaces.

Natasha: Hi, Taku. It's been a long time. (1) _____ _____ _____
_____?

Taku: Hi, Natasha. It has been a while, hasn't it? I've been good, thanks. Life's been busy, but I'd (2) _____ be busy than bored in my apartment all day!

Natasha: Yeah, I agree. What's been keeping you busy?

Taku: I've been doing so much that (3) _____ _____ _____
_____ to start answering that question. One big thing I've done since we last met was getting my driver's license.

Natasha: Wow, congratulations! Was it difficult?

Taku: Not really. I was nervous to begin with, but it didn't take long to relax. Once you get used to what you need to do, it's actually quite easy. Have you started to drive, yet?

Natasha: No, not yet. I want to go to a driving school someday soon, but I can't
(4) _____ it right now.

Taku: Why's that? You haven't been spending (5) _____ _____
_____ _____ on guitars again, have you?

Natasha: No, but I am saving up to buy a keyboard. I want to start a band with my friends and I'm the (6) _____ guitar player out of all of us. I can't sing and I'm definitely not going to start playing the drums, so it has to be the keyboard for me.

Taku: You were always (7) _____ _____ _____ the keyboard anyway. I thought you were pretty good at playing the guitar, too, though. Are you starting the group with friends from the new college you started?

Natasha: No, these guys are from my local gym. We all met last year when we were trying kickboxing for the first time.

Taku: Nice! Musical and strong! Well, if you need (8) _____ to drive you to the music venues you play at, let me know.
I could even be your manager!

Speaking Practice: Practice the conversation with your partner.

IV ‖Pronunciation Check

リダクション：消える音 g

これまで t や p の音が消えるリダクションについて学んできました。それ以外に g の音にもリダクションが起こることがあります。特に進行形などの -ing で終わる場合、最後の g の音ははっきりと発音されません。カジュアルな言い方として、coming を comin' のように最後の g をアポストロフィで省略した表記をすることもあります。また、unloading goods のように、g が続くときには最初の語の g の音が消えているように聞こえます。

Exercises

 53

■ Listen to the recording and choose the sentence which uses reduction, A or B. Then, practice saying the sentences, paying attention to reduction.

1. I met him at the park a long time ago.   A   B

2. What are you thinking about?   A   B

3. On the day of the big game, he changed his style of playing.   A   B

V ‖Focus on Function

I'd rather be busy than bored. 「退屈するより忙しいほうが良い」

副詞の rather を使って「（〜するより）むしろ〜したい、〜したほうが良い」という表現ができます。would rather do の形で、会話では I would は I'd と省略されることがあります。具体的に何かと比較するときには "I would rather eat meat than fish." のように than を後ろに付けますが、必要がない場合は than 以下を省くことが多いです。否定の用法では would rather not で「むしろ〜したくない」の意味を表します。

Exercises

■ Complete the sentences below using *would rather*.

1. フランス料理より和食が食べたいな。
   _____ _____ have Japanese food _____ _____ .

2. **A:** You have many brothers. It looks like a lot of fun!
   B: _____ _____ live _____ . （一人暮らしのほうが良いよ）

3. **A:** Would you like to eat out tonight?
   B: Sorry, I _____ _____ _____. （むしろ行きたくないな）
   I'm not feeling well today.

VI Find out

In the conversation on p.76, Natasha and Taku talked about things they have done recently. Think about an activity you have done recently or would like to do. Then, write the questions below. Next, write your answers to the questions. Finally, ask a partner the questions and find out what the activity they have done or would like to do is.

The activity you have done recently or would like to do: _____

Q1: (expensive) _____?

You: _____ | Your partner: _____

Q2: (need to / travel) _____?

You: _____ | Your partner: _____

Q3: (need / training) _____?

You: _____ | Your partner: _____

Q4: (do / alone) _____?

You: _____ | Your partner: _____

Q5: Your question: _____?

You: _____ | Your partner: _____

The activity your partner has done recently or would like to do: _____

Useful Language

Noun phrases: license / equipment / skill / practice / trial / procedure / convention
Verb phrases: participate / cost / invite / recommend / prepare / join / keep -ing / regret
Adjectives: reasonable / special / difficult / simple / enjoyable / thrilling / practical / frightened

《相手にも薦めてみよう》
今まで経験したもので相手にも薦めたいときは、"I recommend you . . ."と言ってみましょう。
"You should . . ."の言い方もできます。「やるだけの価値がある」は、"It is (really) worth doing."
と言います。do の部分を別の動詞に置き換えることもできます。答えるときは、"I really want
to . . ."や"I'd love to . . ."など「ぜひやってみたい」という表現を使ってみましょう。

UNIT 14

I'm at work.
– Talking about Work and Jobs

I Vocabulary

Part 1: Match the words and phrases (a~j) with their meanings (1~10).

a. salary	b. client	c. quit	d. transfer	e. interview
f. staff	g. meeting	h. get in touch	i. run over	j. colleague

1. _____ to go beyond a limit
2. _____ to move to a different place or job for the same employer
3. _____ a person who works with you
4. _____ a formal meeting with someone who is being considered for a job or other position
5. _____ an amount of money that an employee is paid each week, month, or year
6. _____ a group of people who work for an organization or business
7. _____ a person who pays a professional person or organization for services
8. _____ to communicate with another person especially by calling or writing
9. _____ to leave a job, school, career, etc.
10. _____ a gathering of people for a particular purpose

Part 2: Complete the dialogs with words and phrases from Part 1.

1. **A:** Hi, John. I'm calling you about tomorrow's party.
   B: Sorry, Tom. I'm at work, so I can't talk right now. I'll _____ with you later.
2. **A:** How was your job _____, Urara?
   B: I don't know. They asked me some very difficult questions. I hope they give me a job though because I really want to work there.
3. **A:** Oh, no. It's Mr. Tanaka from Hypersonic Audio.
   B: What's wrong? Hypersonic Audio is our best client.
   A: I know, but meetings with Mr. Tanaka always _____ by a lot.
4. **A:** Why did you _____ your job?
   B: Well, the salary was good, but I just didn't enjoy working there.
5. **A:** Why did you decide to work for a company in Hokkaido? I thought you hated cold places.
   B: I do. And the pay isn't very high, either. But every member of staff has the chance to _____ to the office in Hawai'i. This time next year, I'll be surfing in Maui!

🔲 **Listening Practice:** Listen to two people talking about their jobs. Write the jobs and check (✔) the correct boxes.

1. Job: _____

	Yes	No
has just started	☐	☐
has a good salary	☐	☐
enjoys the job	☐	☐
has nice colleagues	☐	☐

2. Job: _____

	Yes	No
has just started	☐	☐
has a good salary	☐	☐
enjoys the job	☐	☐
has nice colleagues	☐	☐

🔲 **Speaking Practice:** Which of the following aspects of work are important to you? Check the boxes below and talk to your partner about work and jobs.

	Very important	Quite important	Not important	Reason
the location	☐	☐	☐	_____
the salary	☐	☐	☐	_____
interesting work	☐	☐	☐	_____
nice colleagues	☐	☐	☐	_____
nice customers/clients	☐	☐	☐	_____

Useful Language

Questions
- What kind of work do you want to do?
- What is important to you when you get a job?
- Do you have a part-time job?

Answers
- I want to become . . .
- XX is important to me because . . .
- Yes, I do. / No, I don't.

Details
- Occupations: doctor / artist / chef / lawyer / farmer / fisherman / conductor / nurse / public official / bank clerk / tour guide / engineer / journalist

Notes

I have a part-time job.
「アルバイトをする」は、"do a part-time job" または "work part-time" と表現します。日本語のアルバイトは、ドイツ語の Arbeit に由来する言葉で、英語ではないので、気をつけましょう。「バイトがある」は "I have a part-time job." と言います。常勤の仕事は "a full-time job" になります。

III | Conversation

 CD 56

Part 1: Listen to the conversation and choose the most appropriate answer (a~d) for each question.

Get the gist

1. What can we infer about Erik and Helen?
   a. They are both university students.
   b. They are both going to the US.
   c. Neither of them were on time for their meeting.
   d. Neither of them like their manager at work.

2. Who are Erik and Helen most likely?
   a. Friends
   b. Co-workers
   c. Manager and employee
   d. Interviewer and interviewee

Get the details

1. What is most likely Helen's job?
   a. She is a teacher.
   b. She is a lawyer.
   c. She is a server.
   d. She is a game designer.

2. How does Erik most likely feel about his job?
   a. Sad
   b. Angry
   c. Happy
   d. Tired

3. Which of the following is true about Erik?
   a. He is being transferred to the US.
   b. He does not like his manager.
   c. He is doing his dream job.
   d. He quit his job recently.

4. Which of the following is true about both Helen and Erik?
   a. They work at the same company.
   b. Erik was Helen's first manager.
   c. They graduated recently.
   d. They are looking for new jobs.

5. Why did Helen resign from her job?
   a. Because she wants to be a lawyer.
   b. Because she was too busy.
   c. Because her job was to make tea.
   d. Because her boss changed.

Part 2: Listen to the conversation again and write the missing words in the spaces.

Erik: Hi, Helen. I'm sorry I'm so late. Were you waiting long?

Helen: No worries, Erik. I only got here (1) _____ _____ _____ _____ myself. So, we were both late! Anyway, how are you? I can't believe it's been nine months since we (2) _____.

Erik: You're right. It's only been nine months. I've been so busy at work that university life (3) _____ _____ _____ _____ years ago.

Helen: Oh, that doesn't sound good. Aren't you enjoying your job?

Erik: I love it! Being a lawyer is what I've wanted to do since I was in (4) _____ school. It's so interesting, and I really feel that I'm helping to make people's lives better. The only problem is that it's difficult to find the time to do anything else. That's why I was late today. I was with a client at my office, and the meeting ran over time.

Helen: Well, I'm (5) _____ _____ _____ _____ you're enjoying your work. But you need to make sure you don't overdo it and find time to rest and relax.

Erik: That's why I'm here! How are you finding your job, Helen?

Helen: I quit.

Erik: What?! Why?! I thought you really liked working at that company.

Helen: It was great at first, and the pay was really good. My manager was really kind and helpful, and I learned a lot from her. But she (6) _____ to the US after a couple of months, and we got a new manager. He was terrible. He made lots of mistakes, got angry easily, and kept telling me to make him some tea! But my job was to design games, not make tea. So, I resigned. That was nearly two months ago.

Erik: Oh no, that sounds really bad. But what are you going to do now? Are you looking for a new job?

Helen: I've already got one. When my old boss heard I'd left my job, she (7) _____ _____ _____ _____ me. I had an online interview with her last month, and after that she (8) _____ me a job with her department in the US. That's why I was late, too. I had to get my visa today because I'm leaving next week. Shall we get some champagne to celebrate?

Speaking Practice: Practice the conversation with your partner.

82

IV Pronunciation Check

弱い発音に注意しよう！

Unit 1 で英語の発音には強弱があることを学びました。弱く発音される語の一つに、接続詞があります。and や that は、その後に単語や節が続くことを示すもので弱く発音されます。英語を話すときや聞くときに、これらの接続詞の強さを意識してみましょう。

例）bread <u>and</u> butter［and が弱く発音されます］

I'm glad to hear <u>that</u> you're enjoying your work.［that が弱く発音されます］

Exercises

🗨️ EC 💿 CD 57

📑 **Listen to the recording and write the words you hear. Then, practice saying the sentences, paying attention to stress.**

1. It is _____ said _____ _____ _____ contributes to good health.

2. This restaurant _____ very delicious _____ _____ _____ .

3. I didn't _____ _____ Shelly quit her job _____ _____ a company.

V Focus on Function

That's why I was late today.「そんなわけで遅れてしまったんだ」

何かの理由を先に示して、その結果や結論を表現するときには、関係副詞 why を使って、That's why . . . の形で表すことができます。「だから～なのです」、「そういうわけで～なのです」という意味になります。後ろには主語・動詞と文章が続くので覚えておきましょう。本来は That's the reason why S ＋ V の形ですが、the reason が省略されて使われることが多いです。

Exercises

📑 **Look at the sentences below and write a reply using the specified words and *That's why*.**

1. **A:** He is really good at drawing and he loves reading comics. (wants, cartoonist)
   B: _____

2. **A:** I worked the night shift and haven't been back home yet. (tired, today)
   B: _____

3. **A:** Naomi is a talented player. (I think, win the competition)
   B: _____

VI | Find out

In the conversation on p.82, Erik and Helen talked about their jobs. Think about a job that you would like to do. Then, write the questions below. Next, write your answers to the questions. Finally, ask a partner the questions and find out what the job they would like to do is.

The job you would like to do: _____	
Q1: (Where / want / work) _____ ?	
You: _____	Your partner: _____
Q2: (Who / work / with) _____ ?	
You: _____	Your partner: _____
Q3: (What / would / do) _____ ?	
You: _____	Your partner: _____
Q4: (Why / want / do) _____ ?	
You: _____	Your partner: _____
Q5: Your question: _____ ?	
You: _____	Your partner: _____
The job your partner would like to do: _____	

Useful Language

Noun phrases: commuting time / boss / position / employer / employee / career / skill / staff

Verb phrases: work at (in) / work as / promote / create / look for / require / need

Adjectives: international / domestic / public / private / rewarding / responsible

《やりたい仕事について話してみよう》

自分に合う仕事は何だと思いますか？「〜を生かせる仕事につきたい」と言うには、"I want to get a job where I can use . . ." という表現が使えます。「学んだことを生かして」は "apply what I have learnt"、「特技を生かして」は "use my (special) talent to the full" と言います。

UNIT 15

Let's Meet in Paris!
– Talking about Future Plans

I Vocabulary

Part 1: Match the words and phrases (a~j) with their meanings (1~10).

a. target	b. dream	c. schedule		d. upcoming	e. impossible
f. postpone	g. attend	h. look forward to		i. secret	j. organize

1. _____ not able to be done
2. _____ an ideal or perfect aspiration or ambition
3. _____ unrevealed, confidential, classified
4. _____ to be pleased or excited about something that will happen
5. _____ to arrange for something to occur later than originally planned
6. _____ to make arrangements or preparations
7. _____ a timetable of events or activities
8. _____ a goal or objective which someone works towards
9. _____ to be present at an event or meeting
10. _____ planned, going to happen

Part 2: Complete the dialogs with words and phrases from Part 1.

1. **A:** If you could go anywhere in the world, where would you go?
   B: Oh, that's a tough one! Well, it's always been my _____ to see the Pyramids, so I'd go to Egypt.
2. **A:** I got an email from the conference organizers. It's been postponed.
   B: That's a shame. Don't worry, I'm sure they'll offer you the chance to _____ another one in the future.
3. **A:** I'm really _____ Steve's surprise party this weekend.
   B: I know! Me, too! Let's hope that everyone can keep it a secret until then.
4. **A:** What's your _____ for the upcoming year, Julian?
   B: I've got two main ones actually. One's running 5 km in under 19 minutes, and the other is asking you out on a date.
5. **A:** I haven't seen you for a while, Alison. What have you been up to?
   B: A lot! That's why you haven't seen me. My _____ has been packed full!

58, 59

🗨 **Listening Practice:** People are talking about things they plan to do. Write the plans and check (✔) the correct boxes.

1. Plan: _____

	Yes	No
has made arrangements	☐	☐
is expensive	☐	☐
wants to do it for fun	☐	☐
it will help in the future	☐	☐

2. Plan: _____

	Yes	No
has made arrangements	☐	☐
is expensive	☐	☐
wants to do it for fun	☐	☐
it will help in the future	☐	☐

🗨 **Speaking Practice:** What do you think is important to consider when planning something? Check the boxes below and talk to your partner about making plans.

	Very important	Quite important	Not important	Reason
the cost	☐	☐	☐	_____
how long it will take to plan	☐	☐	☐	_____
safety	☐	☐	☐	_____
travel / transport	☐	☐	☐	_____
what to wear	☐	☐	☐	_____

Useful Language

Questions
- Are you good at making plans?
- What are you planning to do on vacation?
- How will you achieve your goal?

Answers
- Yes, I am. / No, I'm not.
- I'm planning to . . .
- First, I'm going to . . . . Next, I'll . . .

Details
- Plans: traveling abroad / learning a language / obtaining a qualification / saving money / buying something / learning to play a musical instrument

Notes

She will carry out her plan.
「計画を実行する」は "carry out" や "execute" という表現を使います。「計画どおりに」は、"as planned" や "according to plan" と言います。
例）"Everything went according to plan."（全て計画どおりにいった）

III Conversation

CD 60

Part 1: Listen to the conversation and choose the most appropriate answer (a~d) for each question.

Get the gist

1. Where are Charlie and Cleo most probably?
   a. At home   **b.** In a restaurant
   c. At university   **d.** In a shop

2. What are they mainly talking about?
   a. Cleo's room   **b.** Projects
   c. Organizing schedules   **d.** Their future plans

Get the details

1. What does using color help stop Charlie becoming?
   a. Organized   **b.** Serious
   c. Confused   **d.** Busy

2. What color would Charlie use to write an assignment deadline in?
   a. Black   **b.** Blue
   c. Red   **d.** Green

3. How does Cleo describe Charlie's advice about making short-term goals?
   a. Impossible   **b.** Easy
   c. Difficult   **d.** Reasonable

4. How did Charlie learn about managing tasks?
   a. By writing long lists   **b.** By doing research into it
   c. By doing breathing exercises   **d.** By taking walks

5. What does Cleo want to become?
   a. A personal assistant
   b. A boss
   c. Serious
   d. Better at planning

Part 2: Listen to the conversation again and write the missing words in the spaces.

Charlie: Hey, Cleo. What's up with your room? Why is there so much paper
(1) _____ ? It looks like a disaster in here.

Cleo: Oh, Charlie, it's awful. I feel like I'm being buried under a mountain of paper
and things to do. I'm (2) _____ _____ _____ all of my
projects and work out what I need to do. But there are so many, it just feels
impossible.

Charlie: Have you tried thinking about colors?

Cleo: What do you mean? How could that help? I'm being serious, Charlie!

Charlie: So am I. Look. This is my (3) _____ . When I have lots of things to do,
I use colors to help me organize them. That way I can write everything I need
to do on one timetable without getting confused. Black is for work, blue is for
university, red is for my club activities, and green is for meeting friends.

Cleo: OK, sorry. That does look easier to read and clearer than (4) _____
_____ _____ _____ . I've just been writing long lists.
Seeing everything on a schedule and timetable like that does look like it'd help.

Charlie: Another thing I do is I try to split my long-term plans up and make shorter-term
goals that are easier to (5) _____ . Things don't seem so difficult then.

Cleo: Well, that sounds reasonable, too. I'll give it a try. (6) _____ _____
_____ _____ so much about this?

Charlie: I looked into it and then (7) _____ out what worked well for me. You
should also do breathing exercises and take walks to relax. I find that helps me
be more productive so I can achieve more when I do sit down to work.

Cleo: I'm not so sure about the walks, but everything else sounds like good advice.
Hey, you're so well-organized, have you ever thought about becoming someone's
personal assistant?

Charlie: Ha! No! I'm going to be the boss, not the assistant. Well, (8) _____
_____ _____ anyway.

Cleo: Good luck! My plan is become better at planning
my plans!

Speaking Practice: Practice the conversation with your
partner.

IV ⫼ Pronunciation Check

英語を聞いたり話したりするとき、主部、述部、句、節などが一つのまとまりとして発音されることに注意しましょう。特に長い文章の場合は、区切る場所を意識すると、内容も理解しやすくなります。

例）Another thing I do / is I try to split my long-term plans up / and make shorter-term goals / that are easier to achieve. [スラッシュの前まで一息で発音します]

Exercises ╱

 61

📢 Listen to the recording and separate the chunks in the sentences below using a slash (/) in the right places. Then, practice saying the sentences, paying attention to chunking.

1. His dream is to become a football player in the Premier League.

2. I saw two women who were talking loudly at the café.

3. The great advantage of this plan is that we can choose from various options.

V ⫼ Focus on Function

I feel like I'm being buried under the paperwork. 「書類の下に埋もれている気がするよ」

「〜の気がする」、「〜と感じる」という表現は、会話の中でよく使われます。そのようなときには、feel like ＋主語＋動詞の形で表しましょう。ここで気をつけたいのは、feel like -ing との違いです。こちらは「〜したい」という意味になります。"I feel like (having) a coffee." （コーヒーが飲みたいです）このような文章では、having が省略されることもあります。

Exercises ╱

📢 Complete the sentences below using *feel like*.

1. 私たちのプロジェクトはうまくいっている気がする。
   I _____ _____ our project is going well.

2. 彼は一日がとても早く過ぎた気がした。
   He _____ _____ the day had passed very quickly.

3. 今日は何もしたくない。
   I _____ _____ _____ _____ anything today.

VI │ Find out

In the conversation on p.88, Charlie and Cleo talked about managing plans. Think about a plan or goal you have. Then, write the questions below. Next, write your answers to the questions. Finally, ask a partner the questions and find out what their plan or goal is.

The plan or goal you have: _____
Q1: (need / travel) _____?
You: _____ │ Your partner: _____
Q2: (done / before) _____?
You: _____ │ Your partner: _____
Q3: (long-term / short-term) _____?
You: _____ │ Your partner: _____
Q4: (easy / to plan) _____?
You: _____ │ Your partner: _____
Q5: Your question: _____?
You: _____ │ Your partner: _____
The plan or goal your partner has: _____

Useful Language

Noun phrases: aim / purpose / preparation / equipment / progress / process / vision / target

Verb phrases: prepare / arrange / start / attempt / carry out / postpone / attend / look forward to

Adjectives: necessary / bright / careful / effective / clear / hopeful / primary / realistic

《計画について話してみよう》

これからやりたいことはありますか？　目標を決めたら、準備と達成するための計画を立ててみましょう。arrange は「準備する、手配する」という意味で、"We are arranging a party." （パーティーの準備をしている）のように使います。prepare も「準備する」という意味で、"I have to prepare the equipment for the trip." （旅行の支度をしなくてはならない）といった使い方をします。

Appendix

Further Practice for Speaking and Writing

It's good to meet you. – Introducing Yourself

Interview your classmates. Speak to at least two people.

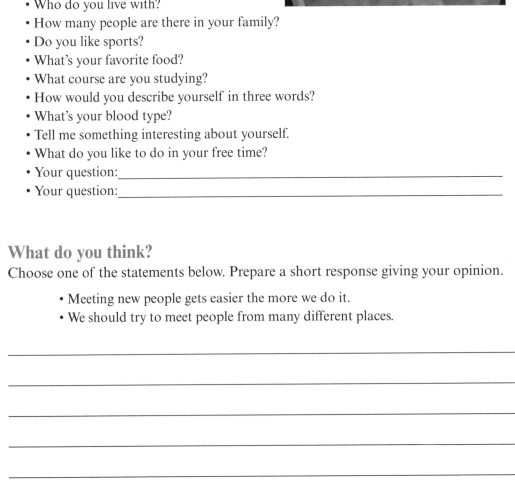

- What's your full name?
- What does your name mean?
- Do you have a nickname?
- Where were you born?
- Where did you grow up?
- Where do you live now?
- Who do you live with?
- How many people are there in your family?
- Do you like sports?
- What's your favorite food?
- What course are you studying?
- How would you describe yourself in three words?
- What's your blood type?
- Tell me something interesting about yourself.
- What do you like to do in your free time?
- Your question:_____
- Your question:_____

What do you think?

Choose one of the statements below. Prepare a short response giving your opinion.

- Meeting new people gets easier the more we do it.
- We should try to meet people from many different places.

_____

_____

_____

_____

_____

What are you into? – Talking about Hobbies and Interests

Interview your classmates. Speak to at least two people.

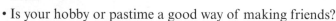

- What is your hobby or pastime?
- How often do you do your hobby or pastime?
- How much time do you spend doing your hobby or pastime?
- Who do you do your hobby or pastime with?
- Is your hobby or pastime a good way of making friends?
- Do you prefer doing things alone or with other people?
- Why do you think some people like dangerous hobbies and pastimes?
- Do you think you will continue to do your hobby or pastime in the future?
- What did you use to like doing when you were younger?
- Do you enjoy doing the same things as other people in your family?
- Have you ever been a leader or manager of a club, circle, or group?
- Do you think students should be able to do more than one club activity?
- Do you have any friends that have very different interests from you?
- Which hobbies or pastimes do you think are the most difficult?
- Do you think people spend too much money on their hobbies and pastimes?
- Your question:_____
- Your question:_____

What do you think?

Choose one of the statements below. Prepare a short response giving your opinion.

- Having a hobby is a great way to reduce stress.
- Hobbies can help us to achieve our dreams.

_____

_____

_____

_____

_____

Who're they? – Talking about Friends and Family

Interview your classmates. Speak to at least two people.

- Is your family big or small?
- How many cousins do you have?
- Who do you get on with best in your family?
- What do you like to do with your family?
- Where do you think the best place to raise a family is?
- Do you have any pets?
- How did your parents meet?
- Are your parents strict?
- What was the most important thing your parents taught you?
- Do you think your parents understand you?
- Who are more important, friends or family?
- Do you make friends easily?
- What qualities do you think are important in a friend?
- Who is your most interesting friend?
- Do you ever argue with your friends?
- Your question:_____
- Your question:_____

What do you think?

Choose one of the statements below. Prepare a short response giving your opinion.

- Children should help with the housework.
- Families should eat dinner together.

_____

_____

_____

_____

_____

Unit 4:

What shall we watch? – Talking about Movies and TV

Interview your classmates. Speak to at least two people.

- What's your favorite movie?
- Who is your favorite movie star?
- Which movie star would you most like to meet?
- Do you choose to watch a movie because of the plot/story or the actors?
- Do you think there is too much violence in movies?
- When was the last time you went to the movie theater?
- How often do you rent movies?
- Has a movie ever made you cry?
- Would you like to be a movie extra?
- Are there any kinds of TV shows that you don't like?
- Who is your favorite TV celebrity?
- Do you prefer to watch TV alone or with other people?
- Do you watch the news on TV?
- Did you watch TV yesterday?
- How many TVs are there in your home?
- Your question:_____
- Your question:_____

What do you think?

Choose one of the statements below. Prepare a short response giving your opinion.

- Movies should be used more for education in schools.
- The amount of TV that children watch should be limited.

_____

_____

_____

_____

_____

What are you listening to? – Talking about Music

Interview your classmates. Speak to at least two people.

- What kind of music do you like?
- Is there any kind of music you hate?
- How often do you listen to music?
- How much time do you spend listening to music?
- When do you like to listen to music?
- What is one of your favorite songs?
- Do you like watching music videos?
- Which do you prefer, songs in English or songs in your own language?
- Have you ever been to a concert?
- Are you a good singer?
- Can you play any musical instruments?
- Do you like to dance?
- Is the image of the group or singer more important than the music?
- Why is music so important to people and culture?
- What are some special or traditional musical instruments in your country?
- Your question:_____
- Your question:_____

What do you think?

Choose one of the statements below. Prepare a short response giving your opinion.

- All students should learn to play a musical instrument at school.
- Musicians have too much influence on young people.

_____

_____

_____

_____

_____

What are you reading? – Talking about Books

Interview your classmates. Speak to at least two people.

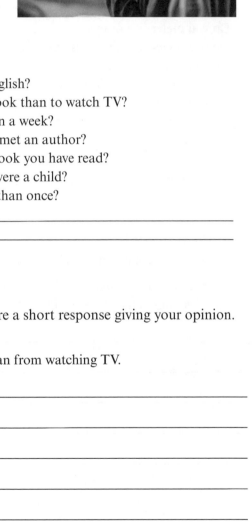

- What is your favorite story or book?
- Who is your favorite author?
- What is your favorite genre of books?
- What is the longest book you have ever read?
- What is the funniest book you have ever read?
- What is the strangest book you have ever read?
- How many books do you own?
- Do you listen to music while you read?
- Have you ever tried to read a book in English?
- Do you think that it is better to read a book than to watch TV?
- How many hours do you spend reading in a week?
- Have you ever been to a book signing or met an author?
- Do you often watch movies based on a book you have read?
- What was your favorite book when you were a child?
- Is there a book that you have read more than once?
- Your question:_____
- Your question:_____

What do you think?

Choose one of the statements below. Prepare a short response giving your opinion.

- Reading books is boring.
- People learn more from reading than from watching TV.

_____

_____

_____

_____

_____

I'm hungry! – Talking about Food

Interview your classmates. Speak to at least two people.

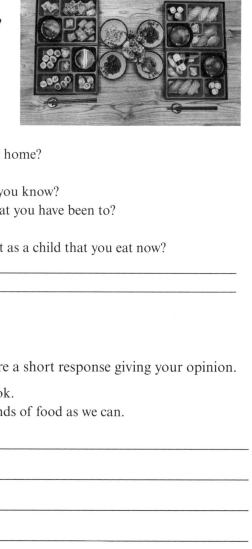

- Are you a good cook?
- Do you eat fruit every day?
- How much does your lunch usually cost?
- What do you eat when you feel sad?
- Do you ever skip breakfast?
- Do you like to try new kinds of food?
- How long do you take to eat lunch?
- Have you ever been on a diet?
- Do you prefer fish or meat?
- Do you prefer to eat at a restaurant or at home?
- Do you often eat out?
- What is the cheapest place to eat at that you know?
- What is the most expensive restaurant that you have been to?
- Do you have any food allergies?
- Are there any foods that you wouldn't eat as a child that you eat now?
- Your question:_____
- Your question:_____

What do you think?

Choose one of the statements below. Prepare a short response giving your opinion.

- Everybody should learn how to cook.
- We should try as many different kinds of food as we can.

_____

_____

_____

_____

_____

How do you stay fit? – Talking about Health

Interview your classmates. Speak to at least two people.

- Are you healthy?
- How often do you exercise?
- Are you a member of a health spa or gym?
- Do you eat fruit and vegetables every day?
- Do you play any sports?
- Do you prefer team sports or individual sports?
- Who is your favorite sportsperson or athlete?
- Would you rather go swimming or skiing?
- Do you think it is okay to gamble on sports events?
- What is your favorite Olympic sport or event?
- Do you like to watch sports on TV?
- Should motor racing be thought of as a sport?
- What's your favorite Japanese martial art?
- Do you think that you need to lose weight?
- Do you take any dietary supplements?
- Your question:_____
- Your question:_____

What do you think?

Choose one of the statements below. Prepare a short response giving your opinion.

- Playing sports is the best way to make friends.
- Training our body is more important than studying.

_____

_____

_____

_____

_____

I don't feel so good. – Talking about Illness

Interview your classmates. Speak to at least two people.

- Do you catch a cold more than once a year?
- How often do you get a cold?
- Do you go for regular medical check-ups?
- Do you have a lot of stress?
- Do you have any allergies?
- Have you ever broken a bone?
- Have you ever donated blood?
- Are you afraid of needles?
- Have you ever tried any alternative health therapies?
- What's the highest temperature you've ever had?
- Have you ever had bad sunburn?
- Have you ever had a bad toothache?
- Have you ever taken a sleeping pill to get to sleep?
- What do you think is the most serious health problem in Japan?
- Would you like to be a doctor?
- Your question:_____
- Your question:_____

What do you think?

Choose one of the statements below. Prepare a short response giving your opinion.

- It is bad for society that people are living longer.
- All people should donate their organs when they die.

_____

_____

_____

_____

_____

Why do you do that? – Talking about Culture

Interview your classmates. Speak to at least two people.

- What do you think is the most interesting part of your culture?
- Is there anything you don't like about your culture?
- Is there a big difference between regional cultures in your country?
- Are there many people of different cultures in your country?
- Have you ever felt confused by the actions of someone from another culture?
- Who in your culture do you admire most?
- Do you think culture is important?
- If you could change one thing about your culture, what would it be?
- Would you ever marry or date someone from another culture?
- What is considered rude in your culture?
- What advice would you give to a group of people who were visiting your country from overseas?
- What do you think is important when visiting another culture?
- What culture besides your own do you admire?
- Do you want to live in another culture?
- Have you ever experienced culture shock?
- Your question:_____
- Your question:_____

What do you think?

Choose one of the statements below. Prepare a short response giving your opinion.

- Traditional cultures are not important anymore.
- It would be better to have one world culture.

_____

_____

_____

_____

_____

Unit 11:

It's a special day. – Talking about Holidays and Festivals

Interview your classmates. Speak to at least two people.

- What's your favorite holiday or special day?
- Are there any holidays or special days you don't like?
- What do you usually do on your birthday?
- Have you ever bought a Valentine's Day gift?
- Do you ever buy or receive Christmas gifts?
- What do you usually do on New Year's Day?
- What are the most important holidays or special days in your country?
- Do you think it's good to celebrate overseas special days like Halloween?
- What was the last holiday or special day that you celebrated?
- Is there a festival in your hometown?
- Do you enjoy going to festivals?
- What's the biggest festival you have ever been to?
- Do you think local festivals are still important nowadays?
- Are there any festivals that you haven't been to but would like to go to?
- Have you ever been to an overseas festival?
- Your question:_____
- Your question:_____

What do you think?

Choose one of the statements below. Prepare a short response giving your opinion.

- We should focus mostly on our own country's special days and festivals.
- Joining local festivals is important.

_____

_____

_____

_____

_____

Are you going anywhere? – Talking about Travel and Vacations

Interview your classmates. Speak to at least two people.

- Have you ever been abroad?
- What's the best vacation you've ever had?
- Have you ever got lost while traveling?
- What countries would you like to visit?
- Where in Japan would you like to go to?
- What is the most interesting souvenir that you have ever bought?
- Do you prefer active or relaxing holidays?
- What's the most beautiful place you've ever been to?
- Have you ever been traveling alone?
- Did you go on a school trip in junior high school?
- Do you prefer summer vacations or winter vacations?
- Do you prefer to travel by train, bus, plane, or ship?
- What do you think some benefits of travel are?
- Have you ever traveled in business class?
- Do you travel with a lot of baggage or do you like to travel light?
- Your question:_____
- Your question:_____

What do you think?

Choose one of the statements below. Prepare a short response giving your opinion.

- There are more benefits than drawbacks to international travel.
- Everyone should travel abroad at least once before starting university.

_____

_____

_____

_____

_____

I've never done that before. – Talking about Experiences

Interview your classmates. Speak to at least two people.

- Have you ever gone skiing?
- Have you ever slept in a tent?
- Have you ever appeared on a TV show?
- Have you ever had a dream about an exam?
- Have you ever done something that you wish you had not done?
- Have you ever fallen asleep while taking a bath?
- Have you ever forgotten the birthday of someone that is important to you?
- Have you ever lied to your parents?
- Have you ever received a present that you really hated?
- Have you ever laughed until your stomach hurt?
- Have you ever received a love letter?
- Have you ever sung in public?
- Have you ever been to a wedding?
- Have you ever walked into something because you weren't paying attention?
- Have you ever got angry on public transportation?
- Your question:_____
- Your question:_____

What do you think?

Choose one of the statements below. Prepare a short response giving your opinion.

- I would rather have an interesting experience than buy something new.
- We can learn something from every experience we have.

_____

_____

_____

_____

_____

Unit 14:

I'm at work. – Talking about Work and Jobs

Interview your classmates. Speak to at least two people.

- Do you have a part-time job?
- What kind of work do you want to do in the future?
- What is a job that you wouldn't want to do?
- Have you ever been promoted?
- Would you prefer to work indoors or outdoors?
- Have you ever done any volunteer work?
- Would you like to work in an office?
- Would you like to work from home?
- Would you like to work overseas?
- Which is more important, making lots of money or enjoying your job?
- Would you like to do an internship?
- When you were a child, what did you want to be when you grew up?
- Who among the people you know has the most interesting job?
- Have you ever considered joining the military as a career?
- What is a good age to retire?
- Your question:_____
- Your question:_____

What do you think?

Choose one of the statements below. Prepare a short response giving your opinion.

- To have one job for your whole life is best.
- Everyone should work abroad for one year.

_____

_____

_____

_____

_____

Let's meet in Paris! – Talking about Future Plans

Interview your classmates. Speak to at least two people.

- How will you spend your weekend?
- What is something you want to achieve within the next five years?
- What is a place you would like to visit?
- What is an activity you would like to do?
- What are three things you want to do in the next vacation?
- Are you good at making plans?
- Have you ever failed to complete a plan you made?
- Do you think parents should make plans for their children?
- How do you make plans for what you will do with your friends?
- Who generally makes the plans in your family?
- Which do you think are better, long-term or short-term plans?
- What is the difference between a plan and a dream?
- Do you ever set goals or targets for yourself on New Year's Day?
- Is it important to be ambitious?
- Are plans important in our personal lives or just at work, school, or university?
- Your question:_____
- Your question:_____

What do you think?

Choose one of the statements below. Prepare a short response giving your opinion.

- We need to have a plan to be successful.
- We should have more than one goal or plan in our lives.

_____
_____
_____
_____
_____

TEXT PRODUCTION STAFF

edited by	編集
Takashi Kudo	工藤 隆志
Hiromi Oota	太田 裕美

cover design by	表紙デザイン
Nobuyoshi Fujino	藤野 伸芳

CD PRODUCTION STAFF

narrated by	吹き込み者
Josh Keller (AmE)	ジョシュ・ケラー (アメリカ英語)
Karen Haedrich (AmE)	カレン・ヘドリック (アメリカ英語)

Complete Communication Book 2 – Intermediate –
コミュニケーションのための実践演習Book 2〈中級編〉

2022年1月10日　初版印刷
2023年8月25日　第3刷発行

著　者　James Bury
　　　　Anthony Sellick
　　　　堀内 香織

発 行 者　佐野 英一郎

発 行 所　株式会社 成美堂
　　　　　〒101-0052　東京都千代田区神田小川町3-22
　　　　　TEL 03-3291-2261　　FAX 03-3293-5490
　　　　　https://www.seibido.co.jp

印 刷・製本　萩原印刷株式会社

ISBN 978-4-7919-7242-5　　　　　　　　Printed in Japan